MRCP Part 2 PAEDIATRICS

PRACTICE EXAMS

Deb K. Pal MA MB BChir MRCP(UK)
Senior Registrar
Hospital for Sick Children
Great Ormond Street
London

Paul Gringras MB ChB MRCP(UK)
Senior Registrar
Harper House Children's Service
University College and Middlesex School of Medicine
London

PASTEST

© 1993 PASTEST
Knutsford
Cheshire

First published 1993
Reprinted 1994

ISBN: 0 906896 622

A catalogue record for this book is available from the British Library.

MRCP Part 2 Paediatrics Revision Courses

PasTest Intensive Revision Courses for MRCP Part 2 Paediatrics are designed for candidates who wish to pass first time. These courses take place over two weekends at a convenient centre in central London and are officially approved for study leave under HM 67/27. Our tutors are experienced in membership teaching and give lively exam-oriented sessions based on grey cases, data interpretations and slides from past examinations. Tips on successful exam technique and two mock viva sessions are also included. The pass rate for candidates who have attended PasTest courses is excellent. For full details contact:

**PasTest, Freepost, Knutsford, Cheshire WA16 7BR
Tel: 0565 755226   Fax: 0565 650264**

Text prepared by Turner Associates, Congleton, Cheshire.
Printed and bound by The Cromwell Press Ltd., Wiltshire.

CONTENTS

FOREWORD

It is right that those intending to specialize in paediatrics should have their basic knowledge of the subject tested, so that they, as well as their supervisors and employers, can be reassured that their future is likely to be secure.

The examination for the MRCP can be a formidable hurdle for newly-qualified doctors who are, sadly, often over-worked and short of sleep. The authors of this book have recently surmounted this hurdle and have set out to help others do so as well.

Clear practical guidance on the written parts of the exam is provided. The book also makes a good (and challenging!) read for those who passed it long ago.

Osmund Reynolds

Professor E.O.R. Reynolds FRS
Professor of Neonatal Paediatrics
University College School of Medicine
London WC1

PREFACE

The examination for the diploma of the Royal College of Physicians has been criticised as anachronistic and a poor discriminator of candidates' ability. Yet without it few paediatricians can make progress in their careers.

Studying for the examination can be an arduous task. The pressure of clinical commitments and the few opportunities available for tuition militate against success. We often have to rely on the goodwill of senior colleagues to coach us out of hours. It is in an effort to ameliorate the lot of the student that this book has been conceived.

The completion of this text would not have been possible without the support and cooperation of like minded individuals. In particular we would like to thank Dr. Ed Broadhurst for his critical review in the draft stage.

Bonne chance!

Deb Pal
Paul Gringras

The overall pass rate for the MRCP (UK) Part 2 is about 30% with variation between colleges. The written part of the MRCP is not a simple hurdle into the 'main' clinical section. It is in fact the written section that provides the most scope for maximising your score.

35% of candidates will fail the written section outright and will not qualify to enter for the clinical examination. However, 15% score a '9' or bare fail in the written section and will be allowed to enter the clinical section. A bare fail in the written section must be balanced by 2 extra marks in the clinical section, a daunting task (no official figures available). A fail in the clinical section cannot be offset by high marks in the written section. Thus it is paramount to do well in the written section and to avoid a bare fail.

The MRCP Part 2 Paediatric examination is divided into three parts: case histories or 'grey cases', data interpretation and visual material.

Particular care should be paid to the phrasing of answers.
Abbreviations should be avoided.

- Where a choice is allowed the most relevant investigation should be listed first.
- Poor wording may lose vital marks in this close-marked exam.

Case histories

- There are five of these with unequal weighting.
- The first question is common to the adult MRCP paper and thus usually involves a problem of adolescence such as diabetes, Guillain-Barré etc.
- Neonatology questions are now always represented and require some practical experience of neonatal intensive care.

Data interpretation

- Ten questions are presented.
- ECGs, EEGs, family trees and audiograms are included.

Visual material

These are mostly clinical photographs, although less than half may consist of radiological imaging, blood films etc.

About this book

Questions have been set out in the form of five individual papers with accompanying rubric. Visual material has been omitted owing to the availability of several excellent atlases.

Key points in discriminating information are given and a discussion section outlines current opinion. The explanations aim to provide frameworks for problem solving and pattern recognition.

NORMAL RANGES AND ROUTINE VALUES

This list is by no means intended to replace any of the available lists of normal values and is not comprehensive.

There are, however, various values that the candidate will be expected to know since normal ranges are not provided.

Past questions, for example, have expected the candidate's knowledge of the physiological fall in haemoglobin towards the second week. Other questions have depended on knowledge of normal cerebrospinal fluid indices in the neonate.

HAEMATOLOGICAL VALUES:

AGE	Hb(g/dl)	PCV	MCV(fl)	MCHC(g/dl)	WCC(10^9/l)
Cord blood	13.5-20.0	0.50-0.56	110-128	29.5-33.5	9-30
14 days	14.5-18.0	0.50-0.58	107-121	31-34	6-15
One year	10.5-13.0	0.36-0.40	80-96	32-36	6-15

Serum Iron: 5-25 micromoles/l infants
10-30 micromoles/l children
Ferritin: up to 150 micrograms/l in children
B_{12}: 150-1000 nanograms/l
Folate: 3.0-20 nanograms/ml

Haemostatic Values:
Platelet count: 150-400 10^9/l
Bleeding time: up to 6 mins
Prothrombin time: within 2-3 seconds of control (INR ~ 1)
Partial thromboplastin time: within 6-7 seconds of control

BIOCHEMICAL RANGES

Sodium: 132-145 mmol/l
Potassium: neonate 4.0-7.0
child 3.5-5.5 mmol/l
Urea: 2.5-8.0 mmol/l

Calcium: neonate 1.8-2.8 mmol/l
             child 2.15-2.70 mmol/l
Phosphate: neonate 1.3-3.0 mmol/l
             child 1.0-1.8 mmol/l
Osmolality: 275-295 mOsmol/kg
Thyroxine: infant 90-200 mmol/l
             child 65-180 mmol/l
Thyroid stimulating hormone:child up to 5 mU/l

URINE
Osmolality greater than 870 mOsm/kg after overnight fluid deprivation

CSF
Glucose: 2.5-4.5 mmol/l (Need blood glucose to interpret, should be
          around 75% of blood glucose)
Protein: newborn 0.4-1.2 (g/l)
          neonate 0.2-0.8
          child 0.15-0.45

Mean values of non-infected CSF in young infants*		
CSF fluid parameter	0-4 weeks	4-8 weeks
Leucocyte count (/mm^3)	11.0	7.1
Polymorphs (/mm^3)	2	3
Absolute neutrophil count (/mm^3)	0.4	0.2

*ref: Bonadio WA, Bruce R, Barry D, Smith D
        Paediatric Infectious Disease Journal 1992, 11:589-591

CASE HISTORY PAPER

(Time available: 55 minutes)

1. Answer **all the questions** based upon the following 5 case histories in the spaces provided.

2. When asked (for example) to list 3 diagnoses or investigations, one line will be provided for each answer. If more than the required number of answers are given, the additional answers will not be scored.

Case History 1

A 14 year old girl is investigated for short stature. She was diagnosed as having anorexia nervosa two years ago, soon after her menarche. Since then, despite behavioural and family therapy she has remained anorexic and has been amenorrhoeic for the last year.

On examination she is very thin with dry lips and angular cheilitis. Examination of other systems normal. Blood pressure normal. Urinalysis normal.

Hb 9.9 g/dl
WBC 12.1 x 10^9/l
Platelets 320 x 10^9/l
ESR 40 mm/hr
Na 136 mmol/l
K 3.6 mmol/l
Urea 3.1 mmol/l

Question 1

a) What further investigation would be useful in making a diagnosis?

....

b) What is the most likely diagnosis?

....

Case History 2

A baby is born prematurely at 34 weeks' gestation. He is normal at birth then vomits and at 12 hours is tachypnoeic. Feeds are stopped and he settles with nasogastric feeding. At 3 days of age he becomes apnoeic, is intubated and ventilated. Jerking movements are noted whilst on the ventilator.

Investigations:
    Urea and electrolytes normal
    Blood glucose 2.4 mmol/l
    HCO_3 10 mmol/l
    pH 7.1
    FiO_2 0.28
    PaO_2 10 kPa (arterial)
    $PaCO_2$ 5.1 kPa (arterial
    Base excess = -17 mmol/l
    Chest X-ray normal
    CSF protein 1.4 g/l, glucose 1.9 mmol/l
    CSF WBC 28/mm^3, polymorphs, RBC 44/mm^3
    CSF Gram stain no organisms seen

Cerebral ultrasound shows diffusely increased echogenicity, the ventricles are not clearly seen.

Question 2

a) What is the most useful investigation?

....

b) What is the most likely diagnosis?

....

Case History 3

A nine year old boy presents with a two week history of an unproductive cough and pain over the right chest wall. He has been treated for right lower lobe pneumonia with ampicillin for one week and co-trimoxazole for four days. The child is getting worse with a poor appetite and weight loss, headache and dizziness.

Father is a postman. His mother had pneumonia responding to antibiotics two weeks ago. His seven year old brother is well and the family lives in a two room council flat with a cat and a budgie.

On examination he is pyrexial 40°C and looks ill. Pulse rate 170. He appears mildly dehydrated with signs of recent weight loss. There is reduced movement of the right side of the chest, dull percussion note and reduced breath sounds in the right lower zone accompanied by crepitations. The rest of the examination is normal. Urinalysis is negative.

Investigations:

    Hb 10.9 g/dl   WBC 6.2×10^9/l diff. normal ESR 65 mm/hr
    Reticulocytes 3.5% MCHC 33 g/dl
    Sputum culture mixed growth
    Mantoux test   negative
    Chest X-ray   Right lower lobe consolidation
                      Right costophrenic effusion
    Pleural tap   1 ml clear serous fluid, 2 WBC: culture negative

Question 3

a) What investigations are of most value in diagnosis?

    ....

    ....

    ....

b) What is the drug of choice?

    ....

Case History 4

A 13 year old boy presents with a 3 day history of productive cough with purulent sputum. On several occasions, the cough produced a cupful of bright red blood.

He was well until 2 months previously when he was struck in the chest whilst playing football. He remained breathless for a few hours before recovering.

Two days later whilst sitting at his school desk he had a sudden paroxysm of severe coughing which eventually settled, so he was well on returning home.

One week later he described symptoms of right sided pleuritic chest pain and a cough productive of small amounts of mucoid sputum, stained with flecks of blood.

He was seen in hospital, at that stage apyrexial with a normal white blood count and negative blood cultures. Chest X-ray showed patchy infiltration of the right lower lobe. He was treated with oral erythromycin and responded well clinically and radiologically.

Two weeks later he was admitted again. This time his temperature was 38.5°C, he had bronchial breathing and crackles at the right lung base. The chest X-ray demonstrated consolidation with a possible fluid level in the posterior segment of the right lower lobe.

Question 4

a) What is the most likely diagnosis?

....

b) What is the most important investigation?

....

Case History 5

A two and a half year old caucasian boy was admitted with a history of diarrhoea and abdominal pain.

Over the last three weeks he had been mildly unwell with a cough and cold which had improved over the previous week. Two days prior to admission he had watery green diarrhoea, the last three stools being flecked with fresh blood. The abdominal pain was constant but worse on opening his bowels causing him to cry and draw his knees up.

In the past he had had a tonsillectomy and required tympanostomy for chronic serous otitis media five months previously. His only medication was cough linctus.

On examination he was apyrexial, tired and miserable. He was not clinically dehydrated. Abdomen was generally tender but soft with no palpable masses. The rest of the examination was normal.

Investigations:
    Hb 12.3 g/dl
    WBC 21.9 x 10^9/l
    Platelets 737 x 10^9/l
    Na 135 mmol/l
    K 4.1 mmol/l
    HCO_3 18 mmol/l
    Urea 6.9 mmol/l
    Creatinine 73 mmol/l
    Glucose 4.5 mmol/l

Blood cultures and stool specimens were sent for culture and he was commenced on maintenance intravenous fluids. The next day he continued to have abdominal pain and pass bloody mucous stools. A plain abdominal X-ray with the appearance of fluid levels was followed by a normal barium enema examination.

On the fourth day of admission with no improvement he was noted not to have passed urine for twelve hours. He looked pale and unwell, with slight puffiness of the eyelids and mildly jaundiced sclerae. A fluid challenge was unsuccessful.

Investigations:
    Na 124 mmol/l
    K 5.5 mmol/l
    HCO3 19 mmol/l
    Urea 12.6 mmol/l
    Creatinine 163 mmol/l

Question 5

a) What immediate investigation would you perform?

    ....

b) What additional clinical information is required?

    ....

c) What is the most likely explanation for the deterioration?

    ....

EXAM 1

DATA INTERPRETATION PAPER

(Time available: 45 minutes)

1. Answer **all 10 of the following questions** in the spaces provided.

2. When asked (for example) to list 3 diagnoses or investigations, one line will be provided for each answer. If more than the required number of answers are given, the additional answers will not be scored.

Question 1

A 12 year old African boy is tested for sickle cell disease pre-operatively. His father is known to have sickle cell trait.

Results   Hb 10.1 g/dl
            RBC 6.1 x 10^{12}/l
            MCV 65 fl
            MCH 21.1 pg
            MCHC 30 g/dl
            Sickle test positive
            HbS 71%
            HbA 21.5%
            HbA2 4.5%
            HbF 3%
            Serum ferritin 159 mcg/l

a) What haemoglobinopathy does the boy have?

....

b) What haemoglobinopathy would you expect on testing the mother?

....

Question 2

A boy has the following blood results:

Ca 2.4 mmol/l PO4 0.7 mmol/l Alkaline Phosphatase 360 u/l
Parathyroid hormone normal 25(OH)D3 normal Creatinine normal
Urine pH normal, no glycosuria, no aminociduria

a) What is the diagnosis?

....

Question 3

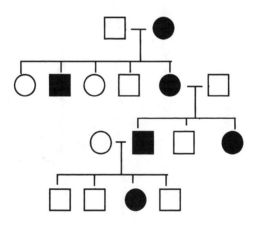

a) What is the mode of inheritance shown?

....

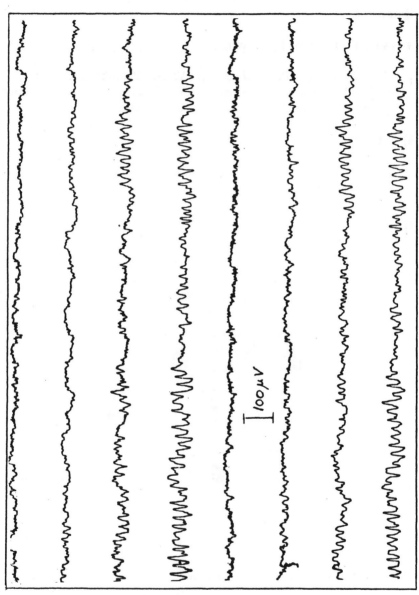

EEG relating to question 4

Question 4

This 12 year old schoolboy is under investigation for frequent 'faints', often occurring early in the morning, and episodes of poor concentration at school. He is right handed and the EEG shown opposite was performed while he was awake.

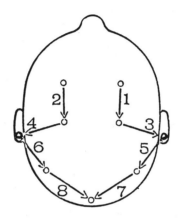

Montage Used

a) What does this EEG show?

....

Question 5

A 9 month old boy is admitted for investigation of failure to thrive and persistent chest infections.

Investigations:
Hb 9.1 g/dl
WBC 12.4 x 10^9/l
Platelets 260 x 10^9/l
Na 126 mmol/l
K 2.0 mmol/l
Cl 82 mmol/l
Urea 4.0 mmol/l
HCO_3 40 mmol/l

Sweat test
Weight of sweat collected 200 mg
Na 75 mmol/l
Cl 82 mmol/l
K 40 mmol/l

a) What is the diagnosis?

....

b) Describe the electrolyte abnormalities.

....

c) What is the cause of these abnormalities?

....

Question 6

An 11 year old boy performed standard spirometry and produced the following results:

	Actual value	Predicted value
FVC (l)	1.13	2.07
FEV_1(l)	1.08	1.87
FEV_1/FVC (%)	95	97
FEF 25-75% (l/sec)	1.89	2.26

a) What type of respiratory impairment is present?

....

b) Give three possible causes for these results.

....

....

....

Question 7

A boy can do the following:

- hold a cup with both hands
- speak in two to three word sentences
- walk up stairs with one hand held
- after several attempts, build a three block tower

a) What is his developmental age?

....

Question 8

A 4 year old girl has a cardiac catheter investigation:

Site	O_2 Saturation(%)	Pressure (mmHg)
SVC	75	4
IVC	74	
RA	75	
RV	90	90/8
PA	90	20/4
LA	90	6
LV	89	92/10
Aorta	80	90/50

a) What two abnormalities are present?

....

....

b) What is the most likely diagnosis?

....

Question 9

Examine the audiogram below.

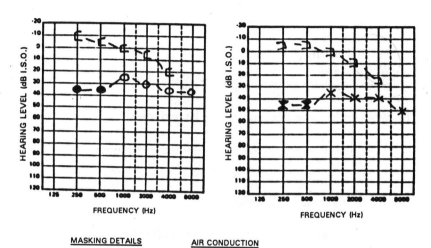

MASKING DETAILS

AIR CONDUCTION

RIGHT   O   LEFT   X

MASKED   ●   MASKED   ✖

BONE CONDUCTION

UNMASKED (RIGHT OR LEFT) ▲

MASKED RIGHT [LEFT]

a) What does it show?

....

b) Give a possible cause for this.

....

Question 10

A 6 day old baby boy was born weighing 3.95 kg. After some mild temperature fluctuation on the first day he is discharged home the following day. On the third day he is readmitted looking very ill and lethargic. He is resuscitated with plasma. Serum electrolytes on admission were as follows:

Na 132 mmol/l
K 4.7 mmol/l
Bilirubin 320 μmol/l
Weight 3.4 kg
Urine osmolality 88 mOsm/kg

a) What further investigation needs to be performed?

....

More detailed studies are carried out:

Serum 17 hydroxy progesterone 2.6 nmol/l (normal < 20 nmol/l)
Plasma renin   high
Plasma aldosterone   low
Plasma ACTH   very high
Plasma cortisol   96 nmol/l

Urine Na   90 mmol/l
24 hour urine steroid profile
     androgens   very low
     cortisol metabolites very low

b) What is the diagnosis?

....

c) How would you treat the child after initial resuscitation?

....

CASE HISTORY PAPER

(Time available: 55 minutes)

1. Answer **all the questions** based upon the following 5 case histories in the spaces provided.

2. When asked (for example) to list 3 diagnoses or investigations, one line will be provided for each answer. If more than the required number of answers are given, the additional answers will not be scored.

Case History 1

A 2 year old girl is brought into casualty having become unsteady an hour before, then very agitated and arching her back.

Her birth history and past medical history are normal. Her parents were away for the weekend and she was staying with her grandmother, who enjoyed looking after her since the recent death of her husband.

On initial examination there were no focal neurological signs, her temperature was 35.5°C and other systems were normal. Subsequently, whilst still in the casualty department, she had three convulsions, affecting the arms and legs symmetrically, each lasting about three minutes.

Investigations:
    Na 135 mmol/l
    K 3.8 mmol/l
    Urea 2.6 mmol/l
    Glucose 5.1 mmol/l
    Ca 2.3 mmol/l
    Albumin 38 mmol/l

    CSF   RBC 1×10^6/l
          WBC 4×10^6/l
          glucose 4.0 mmol/l
          protein 390 mg/l

Question 1

a) What is the diagnosis?

    ....

b) What is the prognosis?

    ....

Case History 2

A 12 year old boy presented with a 2 month history of malaise and weight loss. He had previously been well with no significant past medical history.

He and his family were from Pakistan and the patient had last visited there when he was 10 years old.

His father had a history of asthma and renal stones but otherwise there was no significant family history.

On examination he was thin and febrile 38.5°C. There was no cyanosis or clubbing and his JVP was seen at the level of his jaw. His respiratory rate was 28 per minute and on auscultation, his breath sounds were vesicular. Pulse 85, apex beat not palpable, heart sounds normal. Abdominal examination revealed a 3 cm enlarged, smooth and non-tender liver. Ascites was present, no other masses palpable.

Investigations:
    Hb 12.1
    WBC 6.4 x 10^9/l   polymorphs 60%
                  lymphocytes 25%
                  eosinophils 6%
                  basophils 6%

    ALT 15   Albumin 34   Bilirubin 24
    Prothrombin time 15/12

    Mantoux negative at 1 in 10,000

    Peritoneal aspirate:
        Protein   28 g/l
        Glucose   5.4 mmol/l
        no cells

    CXR: heart size normal, no abnormalities seen

Question 2

a) What two investigations would you do next?

    ....

    ....

b) What is the most likely diagnosis?

    ....

Case History 3

A 9 day old baby boy is admitted with a two day history of diarrhoea and vomiting.

His birth had been normal, birth weight 3.7 kg at term, and initially had bottle fed well. Both parents had recently had viral gastroenteritis.

Whilst in hospital, intravenous fluids were commenced since he continued to vomit. Initial urine microscopy showed haematuria and he became oliguric during the course of the day. Ten hours after admission he had two short generalised convulsions.

On examination he looked pale and clinically dehydrated. He disliked abdominal examination, screaming and drawing his legs up to his chest. A mass was palpable in the right hypochondrium. The rest of the examination was normal.

Investigations:
    Hb 16 g/dl
    WBC 22 x 10^9/l (70% neutrophils)
    Platelets 35 x 10^9/l

    Blood urea 28 mmol/l

Question 3

a) What is the most likely diagnosis?

....

b) Name three useful confirmatory investigations.

....

....

....

c) Give three possible causes for the convulsions.

....

....

....

Case History 4

A 4 month old boy presents with diarrhoea since birth, tachypnoea and a seborrhoeic skin rash. There is no palpable lymphadenopathy. Two siblings died at age one week and four weeks with diarrhoea.

Investigation:
    Chest X-ray interstitial shadowing
    Hb 11.0 g/dl
    WBC 5.1 x 10^9/l
    Eosinophils 35%
    Platelets 255 x 10^9/l
    IgA absent
    IgG low
    IgM low

Question 4

a) What is the underlying disease?

    ....

b) What organism is the likely cause of the pneumonia?

    ....

c) What is the best treatment for the pneumonia?

    ....

Case History 5

A two year old boy presents with recurrent convulsions. He was born by forceps delivery at 2.4 kg. His development has been normal and his immunisations up to date. His parents are both 25 years old and well although father suffered fits until the age of three. The four year old sister is well.

His first attack occurred six months ago following an upper respiratory tract infection associated with fever. Four more attacks have occurred, all in the early morning. The child is said to be irritable before breakfast and possibly a little unsteady on his feet. He is well in between attacks and takes phenobarbitone 30 mg bd.

On examination he is alert and looks healthy. His height and weight are both below the 3rd centile. There is a 3 cm smooth non-tender hepatomegaly but otherwise examination is normal.

Urinalysis is normal.

Investigations:
Na 138 mmol/l
K 4.5 mmol/l
Urea 4.0 mmol/l
Ca 2.25 mmol/l
PO_4 1.2 mmol/l
Alkaline Phosphatase 800 IU
Fasting glucose 1.6 mmol/l
Hb 11.9 g/dl
WBC 6.4 x 10^9/l
Bone age 18 months

Question 5

a) What is the most likely diagnosis?

....

b) What investigation would you do to confirm the diagnosis?

....

EXAM 2

DATA INTERPRETATION PAPER

(Time available: 45 minutes)

1. Answer **all 10 of the following questions** in the spaces provided.

2. When asked (for example) to list 3 diagnoses or investigations, one line will be provided for each answer. If more than the required number of answers are given, the additional answers will not be scored.

Question 1

A 4 year old Indian girl presents with a 4 day history of increasing puffiness around the eyes. Investigations are as follows:

Na 136 mmol/l
K 5.2 mmol/l
Urea 8.1 mmol/l
Protein 42 g/dl
Albumin 26 g/dl
Hb 12.6 g/dl
WBC 10.2 x 10^9/l
Platelets 170 x 10^9/l
Urinalysis pH 6.5
protein + + +
trace blood

a) What is the most likely diagnosis?

....

b) Give four further investigations.

....

....

....

....

c) Outline management in two sentences.

....

....

....

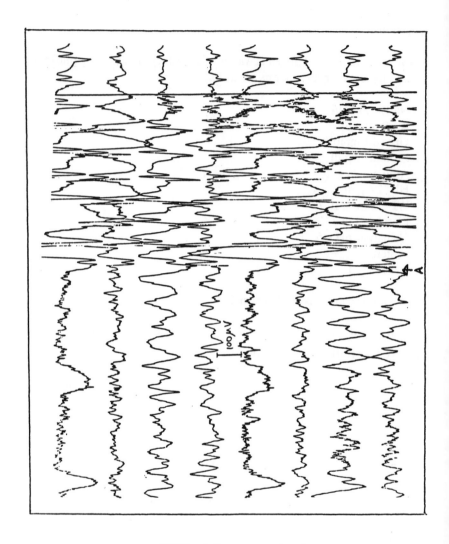

EEG relating to question 2

Question 2

A 6 year old girl is reported by her teacher to have episodic staring spells. During these her facial expression is statue-like and she blinks her eyes. Her physical examination is normal and her EEG is shown opposite.

a) What is the diagnosis?

....

b) What manoeuvre may have been performed at point A?

....

c) Would you perform any further neurological investigations before commencing treatment?

....

Question 3

A baby girl is investigated for prolonged neonatal jaundice. The glucose 6 phosphate dehydrogenase level is found to be subnormal. In addition the mother's G6PD is marginally low whilst father's is normal.

What is the chance of finding a normal G6PD in

a) a male sibling?

....

b) a female sibling?

....

Question 4

A 6 year old boy is investigated for growth failure. Two years previously he had a course of radiotherapy for a medulloblastoma.

Insulin tolerance test

Time (mins)	0	20	30	60	90	120
Glucose (mmol/l)	4.5	1.8	1.6	6.3	7.5	8.1
Cortisol (nmol/l)	508		581	992	741	582
GH (mU/l)	0.9		0.7	1.7	4.2	4.6
TSH (mU/l)	41	>60		>60		
FSH U/l	1.6	>30		>30		
LH U/l	1.2	2.8		3.2		

a) What are the causes of his growth failure?

....

....

....

Question 5

A 10 month old boy from Kenya is referred with failure to thrive. He weighs 4.1 kg and was apparently a normal baby. He is able to sit up if gently supported. He cannot yet crawl or pull himself to standing. He has suffered recurrent otitis media in the last two months despite antibiotic treatment.

Investigations:
    Hb 8.9 g/dl
    WBC 16 x 10^9/l   PMN 50%
                        lymphocytes 40%
                        monocytes 6%
                        eosinophils 1%

    ESR 15 mm/h

    Sickle test negative
    Albumin 23 g/l

    Immunoglobulins   IgG 410 iu/ml (35-115)
                      IgM 236 iu/ml (35-185)
                      IgA 96 iu/ml (10-65)

a) What is the probable diagnosis?

    ....

b) What two tests may help to confirm this diagnosis?

    ....

    ....

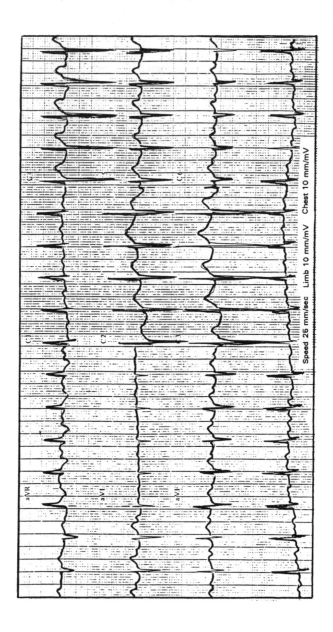

ECG relating to question 6

Question 6

a) Describe three features in the ECG.

....

....

....

b) What is the diagnosis?

....

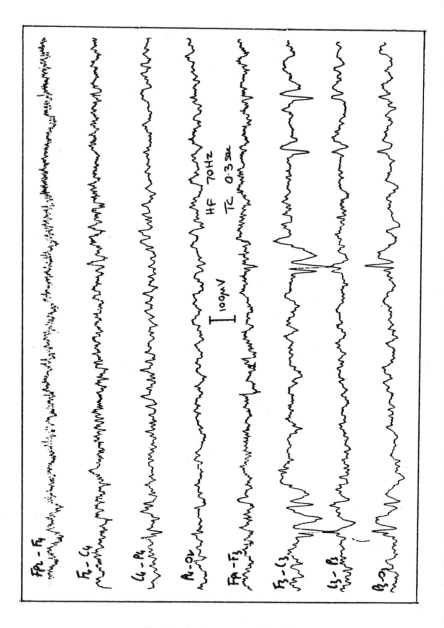

EEG relating to question 7

Question 7

A 9 year old boy is thought to be having night terrors. He has been waking up two hours after falling asleep, making guttural sounds, and one side of his face twitches for about a minute. During this time he understands what is said to him but cannot speak intelligibly. His EEG is shown opposite.

a) Describe any EEG abnormality.

....

b) What is the diagnosis?

....

Question 8

A child with a one-week history of febrile illness treated with ampicillin presents with mild neck stiffness and hemiplegia. CSF results are given:

CSF protein 0.8 g/l
CSF glucose 0.7 mmol/l
CSF WBC 300/mm^3, 68% lymphocytes

Peripheral blood WBC 15 x 10^9/l, 58% lymphocytes

a) What is the diagnosis?

....

Question 9

A 28 week preterm baby is being ventilated for respiratory distress syndrome. The baby is sedated and the ventilator is set at:

Rate   50/min
Pressure   20/3
I:E ratio   1:1
FiO_2 0.8

Arterial blood gases are:

pH   7.15
PaO_2 6.4 kPa
$PaCO_2$ 7.5 kPa
Base excess   -7.1 mmol/l

a) List two ways to improve the ventilation.

....

....

Question 10

A girl with a history of recurrent urinary tract infections presents with renal colic. The plain abdominal X-ray shows calculi in the renal tract.

Na 132 mmol/l
K 3.1 mmol/l
Cl 114 mmol/l
Urea 12 mmol/l

arterial pH 7.23
urine pH 6.6

a) What is the likely diagnosis?

....

b) Give three possible causes.

....

....

....

c) Give two treatment measures.

....

....

CASE HISTORY PAPER

(Time available: 55 minutes)

1. Answer **all the questions** based upon the following 5 case histories in the spaces provided.

2. When asked (for example) to list 3 diagnoses or investigations, one line will be provided for each answer. If more than the required number of answers are given, the additional answers will not be scored.

Case History 1

A 12 year old schoolboy was seen with lower back pain. It began 3 weeks ago during a school P. E. lesson. He initially stayed in bed but despite rest still complained of continual pain. He found walking painful and seemed unsteady on his feet.

His throat had been sore for the past week and his appetite poor. Although he had no dysuria, he complained of frequency and occasional incontinence of urine.

He has been previously well apart from a prolonged chest infection when 10 years old.

On examination he looks unwell, pyrexial 38.0°C. Pale conjunctivae. There is a large unexplained bruise on the right thigh. His throat is red and there are several cervical glands palpable. An enlarged non-tender node is palpable in the left axilla. His back and neck are very stiff, all movements are limited. There is increased tone in both legs. The right ankle jerk is absent but the other tendon reflexes are normal. There is decreased sensation over the dorsum of the right foot.

Question 1

a) What is the most likely diagnosis?

....

b) What two investigations would help confirm the diagnosis?

....

....

Case History 2

A baby is born at 30 weeks gestation and develops respiratory distress syndrome. On day 2 he requires pressures of 24/4, I:E ratio 1:1 and rate of 30 per minute. Blood gas results are satisfactory. Four hours later his clinical condition deteriorates, despite having looking well a few minutes earlier.

Appropriate action is taken and five minutes later the baby is looking well again.

Question 2

a) Give four possible complications of management which may account for the rapid deterioration and recovery.

....

....

....

....

Case History 3

A 6 year old boy is seen by his school doctor. For the last two months he has been off games because of pain in his knees. He has been well before this apart from a fever and headaches two or three months ago. He is fully immunised and has two sisters who are well. His parents are divorced and his mother, whom he lives with, is a fashion designer. She has a history of alcoholism but claims to have been abstinent for three years. The boy is taking 0.5% hydrocortisone cream for a spreading patch of eczema on his trunk and paracetamol for occasional headaches. On questioning, he admits to no particular difficulties at school. His hobbies include constructing aircraft models.

On examination he is shy and pale. Pulse 88, chest and heart normal. Abdomen is soft with 2 cm liver edge palpable on deep inspiration. Both knees appear normal on inspection but slightly painful at the limits of movement. His gait is normal but he finds it difficult to run. The other joints are normal. There is a sacral dimple and, at the waist, an 8 cm erythematous ring with a faded patch in the centre. There is no bruising evident.

Question 3

a) What additional element of the history would you like to elicit?

....

b) How would you make the diagnosis?

....

c) What is your management?

....

....

Case History 4

An 8 year old child with cystic fibrosis presents with gradual onset of generalised abdominal pain and bile stained vomiting over the last two days.

On examination 5% dehydrated, apyrexial. Abdomen moderately distended with generalised tenderness but no guarding. There is a firm mass in the right iliac fossa. The rectum is empty on examination but a mass is palpable in the right iliac fossa.

Question 4

a) Give three differential diagnoses.

   ....

   ....

   ....

b) What investigation would be most helpful?

   ....

Case History 5

A 14 year old girl presents with pain in the lower back and difficulty bending down for the last three days. She thinks her face is swollen and feels weak in her arms and legs. Earlier in the day she had an episode of double vision lasting half an hour. At the age of six she suffered meningitis but made a complete recovery.

On examination she is not breathless or cyanosed. She has no neck stiffness and has an expressionless face. She is unable to close her eyes when asked. Neither can she lift her limbs off the couch. All limb reflexes are absent, the abdominal reflex is present and sensation to light touch is intact.

Investigations:
   Hb 12.6 g/dl
   WBC 5.8 x 10^9/l
   ESR 7 mm/h
   Na 134 mmol/l
   K 5.2 mmol/l
   Urea 5.5 mmol/l
   Creatinine 62 mmol/l

Question 5

a) What is the most likely diagnosis?

....

b) What investigation would you do next?

....

c) How would you monitor her progress?

....

EXAM 3

DATA INTERPRETATION PAPER

(Time available: 45 minutes)

1. Answer **all 10 of the following questions** in the spaces provided.

2. When asked (for example) to list 3 diagnoses or investigations, one line will be provided for each answer. If more than the required number of answers are given, the additional answers will not be scored.

Question 1

A 10 week old baby presents with a two week history of vomiting.

Na 126 mmol/l
K 3.1 mmol/l
Cl 72 mmol/l
Urea 8.4 mmol/l
pH 7.53
HCO_3 45 mmol/l
Glucose 3.6 mmol/l

a) What is the diagnosis?

....

Question 2

Family tree showing affected boy with achondroplasia, normal sister and normal parents.

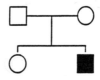

a) What is the risk of a further child being affected?

....

b) What is the risk of the sibling having an affected child?

....

Question 3

A 10 month old obese child presents with hypoglycaemia. There is no ketonuria.

Investigations:

Serum triglycerides raised
Serum cholesterol raised
Plasma glucose (random)   3.0 mmol/l   insulin 25 IU
Plasma glucose (fasting)   1.8 mmol/l   insulin 4.0 IU

a) What is the diagnosis?

....

Question 4

An 11 year old boy with cystic fibrosis complained of a wheeze on exertion. Lung function tests were performed before and 20 minutes after nebulised salbutamol 5 mg:

	Pre	Post	Expected
Forced vital capacity (l)	1.7	1.8	2.1
FEV_1 (l)	1.0	1.5	1.81
Residual volume (l)	1.1	0.9	0.75
Total lung capacity (l)	3.3	3.1	3.0

a) List the three physiological abnormalities these results demonstrate.

....

....

....

b) Name two laboratory techniques that can be employed to measure these lung volumes.

....

....

Question 5

A 13 year old girl is brought for consultation by her mother who believes the girl is not growing. Assessment shows her weight to be increasing satisfactorily and her height to be below the third centile. Her height velocity is falling and she has not entered puberty. Her bone age is 8.28 years.

a) What two investigations would you consider next?

....

....

Combined pituitary function tests are shown below.

Time (mins)	0	20	30	60	90	120
Glucose mmol/l	4.1	0.9	2.1	6.5	8.1	8.7
Cortisol nmol/l	337		797	868	710	640
GH mU/l	0.9		1.4	11.6	4.5	1.0
TSH mU/l	>60	59		>60		
FSH U/l	2.3	6.1		15		
LH U/l	2.0	3.9		45		
PrL mU/l	580	3000		1980		

b) What is the diagnosis?

....

c) How would you treat her and what would you advise the parents?

....

....

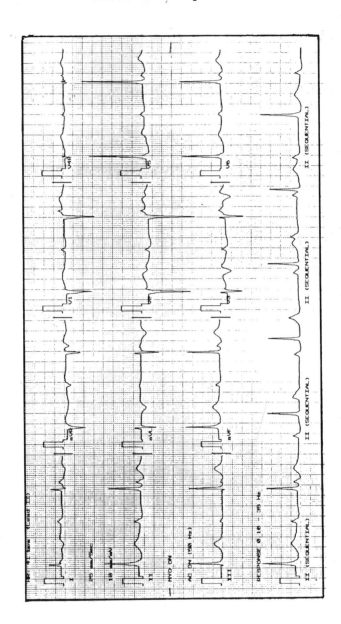

ECG relating to question 6

Question 6

a) What diagnosis can be made from the ECG shown opposite?

....

Question 7

A 7 year old girl with haematuria and purpura has the following blood results:

Hb 6.8 g/dl
WBC 5.0 x 10^9/l
Platelets 15 x 10^9/l

a) Give two possible diagnoses.

....

....

Question 8

A 5 month old infant presents with a vague history of malaise, lethargy and fever for two weeks. On examination he has a macular rash over the body, his hands are slightly oedematous and peeling. His tonsils are enlarged and he has some large lymph nodes in the neck.

Hb 11.1 g/dl
WBC 24.0 x $10^9/l$
Platelets 980 x $10^9/l$
Na 133 mmol/l
K 4.5 mmol/l
HCO_3 18 mmol/l
Urea 3.5 mmol/l
Throat swab no growth
ASOT normal

a) What is the most important differential diagnosis?

....

b) What investigations need to be performed?

....

c) What, if any, treatment should be commenced?

....

Question 9

A boy is asked to copy shapes. He is able to copy a circle and a cross but not a square. When asked to count as far as he can he reaches three. He knows his first name but not his surname.

a) How old is he?

....

b) What would you do next?

....

Question 10

A well 8 week old baby is referred because of pallor noticed in a routine 6 week development clinic. This is the mother's second child and the neonatal period was uneventful.

Investigations:
  Mother's blood group A NEG

  Cord blood
      Hb 16.2 g/dl
      WBC 10.1 x 10^9/l
      Platelets 261 x 10^9/l
      group O pos
      DAT NEG

  at 8 weeks
  Hb 5.1 g/dl
  WBC 12.4 x 10^9/l
  Platelets 321 x 10^9/l

a) Name the three most useful investigations.

   ....

   ....

   ....

b) What is the most likely diagnosis?

   ....

CASE HISTORY PAPER

(Time available 55 minutes)

1. Answer **all the questions** based upon the following 5 case histories in the spaces provided.

2. When asked (for example) to list 3 diagnoses or investigations, one line will be provided for each answer. If more than the required number of answers are given, the additional answers will not be scored.

Case History 1

A 15 year old girl with known complex congenital heart disease is referred to the paediatrician by her general practitioner. Two weeks previously she had complained of increasing shortness of breath and was noted to have an irregular pulse. She is now experiencing chest pain and has coughed up blood stained sputum. She had a repair of her heart defect at the age of eighteen months and has had regular follow up since.

On examination she is cyanosed, has a loud second heart sound and both systolic and diastolic murmurs. Her blood pressure and the rest of the examination are normal.

Question 1

a) What complication of the original lesion has occurred?

....

b) What has precipitated the recent deterioration?

....

c) What was the likely cause of the chest pain?

....

Case History 2

The paediatrician is called to the postnatal ward to examine a six day old baby girl who is jittery and has had a low grade pyrexia over the last 24 hours.

The baby was born, weighing 3.4 kg, by forceps delivery to a 22 year old primigravida. The mother was unbooked and little antenatal history known. At present she is staying with friends in a rented flat. By her estimated dates the baby is 38 weeks gestation.

There was delay in the second stage of labour and a brief type II deceleration on the cardiotocograph trace thirty minutes prior to delivery. Apgar scores of 9 at 1 minute and 10 at 5 minutes were recorded. Since birth she has bottle fed avidly and the midwife observes that she always seems hungry and is difficult to settle to sleep.

On examination her temperature is 37.8°C, weight 3.35 kg and she sucks well. Pulse 180, no murmurs, respiratory rate 40, breath sounds normal. There is no skin rash but she feels sweaty. There are occasional tremulous movements of the arms and legs. Fontanelle is normal and neurological examination is also normal.

Question 2

a) What three immediate investigations would you perform?

....

....

....

b) What is the most likely diagnosis?

....

Case History 3

An 8 year old Bangladeshi boy is sent to hospital by his head teacher. He has been behaving oddly the previous day and today in class was unable to write and displayed jerky movements of his limbs and head. He was taunted in the playground by his friends who thought he was 'mad'. He had been well previously and had not been abroad recently. His birth, development and immunisations in the UK had been normal and he was said to be a difficult child at home. He did well at school and had lots of friends. He was one of nine children, his father a chef and his mother a housewife, living in an old council house. The rest of the family was well. A week ago he had been frightened by a violent neighbour in the street.

On examination he was a well nourished boy, apyrexial. He was fidgety and had continuous, rapid, irregular, jerky movements of the limbs, head and face. These movements ceased when asked to recite the five times table. He was fully orientated with normal higher functions. His speech was dysarthric and explosive. Cerebellar and peripheral nervous system examination was normal. No other abnormalities were found.

Investigations:
  Hb 11.2 g/dl
  WBC 10.8 x 10^9/l
  ESR 48 mm/h
  Na 135 mmol/l
  K 3.4 mmol/l
  Urea 4.3 mmol/l
  Creatinine 43 mmol/l
  HCO_3 22 mmol/l
  Ca 2.1 mmol/l
  PO_4 1.1 mmol/l
  Alkaline phosphatase 410
  AST 54
  Bilirubin 12 μmol/l

  Urinalysis negative

  Lead 1.4 μmol/l
  Toxin screen negative
  Throat swab no growth

Blood cultures no growth

ECG normal
EEG normal
CT brain normal

Question 3

a) What important investigation is missing?

....

b) What is the most likely diagnosis?

....

c) What treatment would you commence?

....

d) What is the prognosis for gait?

....

Case History 4

A baby girl 10 weeks old presents with failure to thrive. The birthweight was 2.3 kg at an ultrasound estimated gestation of 38 weeks. She had passed meconium normally at birth. Maternal health was normal during the pregnancy. The parents are both of short stature and low intelligence.

At 3 weeks she had abdominal distension and Hirschsprung's disease was proven by rectal biopsy. A myomectomy was performed at 5 weeks and the child discharged from hospital at 6 weeks. At 8 weeks the parents noted her to be constipated and refusing to feed. She has not vomited.

On examination she was pale but did not look ill. Her weight was 3.23 kg, temperature 36.4°C, pulse 110 and respiratory rate 32 per minute. She had periorbital oedema and noisy breathing, the nasal airways partially obstructed. She had a large tongue and an umbilical hernia. She was floppy, had no head control and did not smile. The liver was palpable 1 cm below the costal margin but no other organs were palpable in the abdomen.

Urinalysis was normal.

Investigations:
    Hb 10.2 g/dl
    WBC 8.3 x 10^9/l
    Chest X-ray normal

Question 4

a) What one investigation will confirm the diagnosis?

    ....

b) What factors mentioned will influence the mental prognosis?

    ....

    ....

Case History 5

A baby boy aged 6 months was readmitted into hospital. He had spent the first 6 weeks of his life in hospital because of ventricular septal defect and heart failure in the neonatal period. He was treated with digoxin, frusemide and spironolactone and his condition improved by discharge. At that stage his weight, length and head circumference were all between the 10th and 25th centile.

At home feeding time was always difficult but he had progressed to solids and no longer became breathless during feeds. At three months of age he began to have diarrhoea, described as loose and foul smelling, up to 5 times a day.

On admission the baby looked miserable and irritable. Weight (3.0 kg) and length are between the 3rd and 10th centile. He was on digoxin 40 μg daily and frusemide 2 mg bd, spironolactone 2.5 mg bd.

On examination his abdomen was slightly distended with the liver 1 cm below the costal margin. Examination of other systems was normal. Whilst in hospital he continued to have foul smelling, loose stools. Stool culture was negative. After two weeks in hospital he had failed to gain any weight.

Question 5

a) What is the most likely cause of his failure to thrive?

....

b) What is the best investigation to confirm the diagnosis?

....

EXAM 4

DATA INTERPRETATION

(Time available: 45 minutes)

1. Answer **all 10 of the following questions** in the spaces provided.

2. When asked (for example) to list 3 diagnoses or investigations, one line will be provided for each answer. If more than the required number of answers are given, the additional answers will not be scored.

Question 1

A 3 year old girl, previously well, presents with a history of generalised oedema for the last three months, and diarrhoea over the last two months. The diarrhoea is mild and intermittent.

Investigations:
    Urine protein < 30 mg/24 hours
    Albumin 20 g/dl
    Hb 10.2 g/dl
    WBC 4.1 x 10^9/l PMN 60%
                    lymphocytes 10%
                    monocytes   30%

a) What is the diagnosis?

    ....

b) Give two investigations.

    ....

    ....

Question 2

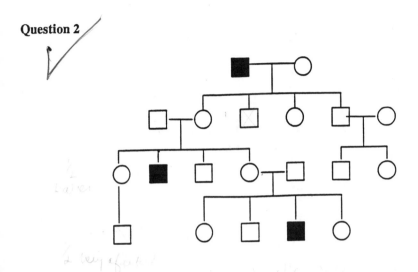

a) What is the pattern of inheritance?

....

b) What is the risk of II3 being a carrier?

....

c) What is the risk of IV1 being affected?

....

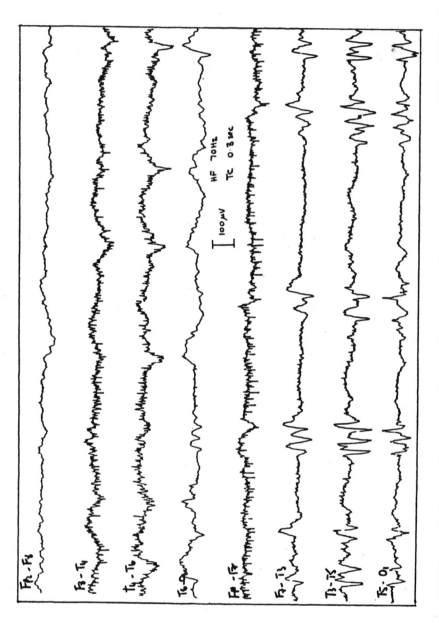

EEG relating to question 3

Question 3

a) What clinical diagnosis would be compatible with this EEG?

....

b) Name one cause.

....

Question 4

A 4 year old girl with no previous history of convulsions is admitted in status epilepticus. The following emergency investigations are performed:

Hb 7.9 g/dl
WBC 6.8 x 10^9/l
Blood glucose 4 mmol/l
Urinalysis protein + + +
Cells none seen
Casts none seen
Clinitest ¾%

a) What is the most likely diagnosis?

....

b) What three investigations would confirm this?

....

....

....

Question 5

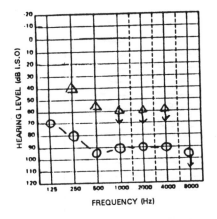
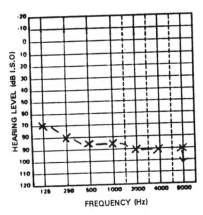

AIR CONDUCTION
RIGHT O   LEFT X

BONE CONDUCTION
UNMASKED (RIGHT OR LEFT) Δ

a) Comment on this audiogram of a 10 year old boy who had meningitis aged 3 years.

....

b) What was the most likely organism?

....

ECG relating to question 6

Question 6

a) What is the abnormality on this ECG?

   ....

b) How would you treat it?

   ....

   ....

Question 7

A 14 year old boy with recent onset of bilateral facial palsy following a febrile illness has this blood count:

Hb 11.2 g/dl
MCV 92 fl
MCH 32 pg
MCHC 34 g/dl
Reticulocytes 5.7%
WBC 16.2 x 10^9/l
PMN 51%
Lymphocytes 49%
Platelets 68 x 10^9/l
ESR 27 mm/h

Blood film atypical cells, spherocytes, agglutination

a) What is the underlying diagnosis?

....

b) How would you confirm this?

....

Question 8

A 6 month old girl is admitted following a febrile convulsion. On the ward she has two further generalised convulsions one hour apart, lasting 2 and 8 minutes. The second seizure is terminated by rectal diazepam.

Investigations:
    Na 137 mmol/l
    K 4.2 mmol/l
    Urea 5.1 mmol/l
    Glucose 3.6 mmol/l
    Hb 12.1 g/dl
    WBC 12.3 x 10^9/l
    Platelets 341 x 10^9/l
    CSF bloodstained
        RBC 12,000 x 10^9/l
        WBC 15 x 10^9/l
    Lymphocytes 80%
    Glucose 3.4 mmol/l unsuitable for protein estimation
    Gram stain no organisms seen

a) What is your immediate management?

    ....

b) What two urgent investigations are necessary?

    ....

    ....

c) What is the likely diagnosis?

    ....

Question 9

A newborn baby was examined at 2 days and was found to have normal femoral pulses. On the third day he became unwell and was noted to have weak femoral pulses. The following cardiac catheterisation data were obtained:

Site	O$_2$ Saturation (%)	Pressure (mmHg)
SVC	55	8
RA	55	8
RV	75	80/8
PA	75	80/50
LA	91	12
LV	91	80/20
Abdom. aorta	85	55/45

a) Give three anatomical abnormalities.

....

....

....

Question 10

A 6 week old baby was born at 32 week gestation after a maternal antepartum haemorrhage. Below are some blood test results:

Hb	8.2 g/dl
MCV	80 fl
MCHC	32 g/dl
Reticulocytes	4%

Blood group O positive
Indirect Coombs test negative
Blood film crenated cells, several spherocytes

a) What is the most likely diagnosis?

....

CASE HISTORY PAPER

(Time available: 55 minutes)

1. Answer **all the questions** based upon the following 5 case histories in the spaces provided.

2. When asked (for example) to list 3 diagnoses or investigations, one line will be provided for each answer. If more than the required number of answers are given, the additional answers will not be scored.

Case History 1

A 13 year old African boy known to have sickle cell disease presents with a 2 day history of intermittent abdominal pain.

He has been admitted on many occasions with acute painful crises and in the last two years has required two exchange transfusions during severe sickle chest syndrome. When last seen in the clinic he was well, Hb 8.1 g/dl and taking regular folic acid and penicillin.

Two days previously, after breakfast he suddenly felt a sharp abdominal pain which made him bend double and later feel nauseated. The pain settled for the rest of the day and he slept well. He was well the following day at school until the afternoon when the pain began again. It was present on admission to hospital and was settling.

On examination he is quite a thin boy, apyrexial and looking comfortable. Sclerae are jaundiced, there is no clubbing or cyanosis. Abdomen is soft and moves with respiration. The liver is just palpable 1 cm below the costal margin. He is tender in the epigastric area and right hypochondrium but there is no guarding. The bowel sounds are normal.

Investigations:
  Hb 8.0 g/dl
  WBC 11.4 x 10^9/l
  Platelets 420 x 10^9/l
  Na 131 mmol/l
  K 4.0 mmol/l

Question 1

a) Give the most likely explanation for his symptoms.

  ....

b) What one investigation would be most helpful?

  ....

Case History 2

A 21 year old pregnant woman is rushed to hospital, in labour. She gives birth, at term, to a baby girl in the ambulance. Mother and child are admitted to the postnatal ward where she begins to breast feed. This is her first baby. At 48 hours the baby is noted to be pale. Mother mentions the passage of dark sticky stools in the nappy. On examination, the baby's pulse is 160, respiratory rate 70, no recession. Stools dark and sticky.

Question 2

a) What two investigations would you perform next?

....

....

b) What would be your immediate treatment?

....

Case History 3

An 11 month old girl presents with a three day history of diarrhoea and vomiting. Over the past 24 hours she has become increasingly lethargic with occasional jerking movements of her lower limbs.

On examination she looked 5-10% dehydrated, drowsy and difficult to rouse. Fontanelle felt full, no neck stiffness, apyrexial, no rash, no lymphadenopathy.

Neurological examination revealed increased tone and brisk reflexes in her lower limbs, plantars equivocal. Fundi normal.

Investigations:
   CSF: RBC $50/mm^3$
        WBC $3/mm^3$ lymphocytes
        no organisms seen
        protein 0.78 g/l
        glucose 2.2 mmol/l

Question 3

a) Give one further investigation that will help to make a diagnosis.

....

b) Give two differential diagnoses.

....

....

Case History 4

A 6 year old girl presents with left lower lobe pneumonia. This responds well to intravenous antibiotics and she is discharged after six days. In her first six years of life she had four episodes of pneumonia, one also in the left lower lobe and the others at different sites. Her first episode was at eighteen months. Between episodes she is active and thriving.

She was born at 39 weeks' gestation and spent twelve hours on the S.C.B.U. with unexplained tachypnoea. This settled, a septic screen was negative and she was returned to her mother.

At three years of age community screening revealed a hearing loss which was due to bilateral serous otitis media. Grommets were inserted.

Question 4

a) What three investigations would you perform?

....

....

....

b) What is the most likely diagnosis?

....

Case History 5

A 13 week old infant is admitted from the child health clinic because of concern over rapid increase in head size. He had been born by forceps delivery at 42 weeks' gestation. There had been some meconium at delivery but the Apgar scores recorded were 7 at 1 minute and 9 at 5 minutes. So far he has been fully immunised and is being bottle fed.

The head size was noted to be above the 97th centile and there were retinal haemorrhages in both fundi. Four small red marks were noticed on the anterior aspect of the chest.

Question 5

a) What is the most likely cause for the increase in head size?

....

b) What three investigations would you perform next?

....

....

....

c) What is your next management step?

....

EXAM 5

DATA INTERPRETATION PAPER

(Time available: 45 minutes)

1. Answer **all 10 of the following questions** in the spaces provided.

2. When asked (for example) to list 3 diagnoses or investigations, one line will be provided for each answer. If more than the required number of answers are given, the additional answers will not be scored.

Question 1

A 5 week old baby presents with a history of vomiting since birth and poor weight gain. On examination he is floppy and lethargic but no other abnormalities are evident.

Investigations
   Na 130 mmol/l
   K 2.0 mmol/l
   Cl 73 mmol/l
   HCO_3 50 mmol/l
   Abdominal ultrasound normal

a) What biochemical abnormality is present?

   ....

b) What investigation should be performed?

   ....

c) What is the most likely diagnosis?

   ....

Question 2

This is the family tree of two families with sensorineural deafness.

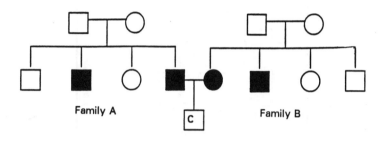

a) What is the inheritance pattern in family A?

....

b) What is the inheritance pattern in family B?

....

c) What is the chance of the offspring indicated having normal hearing?

....

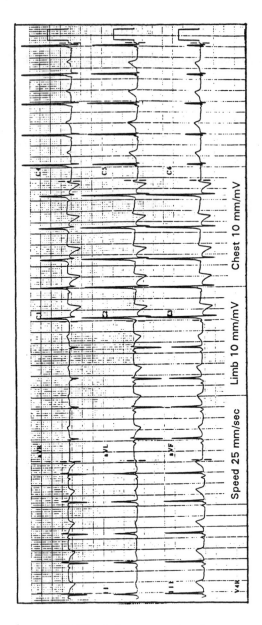

ECG relating to question 3

Question 3

With regard to the ECG shown opposite:

a) What two abnormalities are shown?

....

b) What clinical importance do they have?

....

Question 4

A girl with polyuria has the following serum electrolytes:

Na 145 mmol/l
K 2.8 mmol/l
Cl 95 mmol/l
HCO_3 34 mmol/l
Glucose 6.8 mmol/l

a) Give three possible diagnoses.

....

....

....

Question 5

A 4 year old boy presents with developmental delay. He has mild microcephaly and short palpebral fissures. On cardiovascular examination a soft ejection systolic murmur is heard maximal at the left sternal edge radiating to the carotids.

Biochemistry:

Ca 2.9 mmol/l
PO_4 1.7 mmol/l
Alkaline Phosphatase 113 U/l

a) What is the likely diagnosis?

....

b) What is the cause of the murmur?

....

Question 6

A child can copy the top row of shapes but not the bottom.

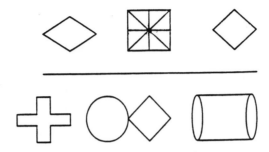

a) How old is he?

....

b) Would you expect him to be able to write his full name?

....

Question 7

The following cardiac catheter data were obtained from a 2 day old infant.

Site	O$_2$ Saturation(%)	Pressure (mmHg)
SVC	63	
IVC	62	
RA	62	mean 4
RV	62	96/5
PA	61	24/5
PV	95	mean 4
LA	80	mean 4
LV	83	90/4
Femoral art.	83	90/55

a) What is the diagnosis?

    ....

b) What immediate treatment should be given?

    ....

c) What is the further management?

    ....

Question 8

A term baby becomes jaundiced at 30 hours of age. The pregnancy and delivery had been uncomplicated.

Total bilirubin 170 μmol/l
Direct bilirubin 10 μmol/l
Hb 15.2 g/dl
WBC 12.1 x 10^9/l
Reticulocytes 5%
Film occasional spherocytes
Blood group A Rh positive
Maternal blood group O Rh negative
Indirect Coombs test positive
Red cell osmotic fragility normal

a) What is the most likely diagnosis?

....

b) Give one further investigation.

....

Question 9

A 2 year old boy was seen with a persistent cough. Examination shows him to be on the 10th centile for weight and height.

Investigations:
Hb 12.0 g/dl
WBC 44 x 10^9/l, 60% lymphocytes, 23% PMN
Platelets 400 x 10^9/l

Chest X-ray patchy opacification right lower lobe

a) What is the diagnosis?

....

Question 10

A 4 day old baby was looking dusky on the post-natal ward. The following were the blood gas results:

	Air	_90% oxygen for 10 minutes_
PaO_2, kPa	6.95	18.6
$PaCO_2$, kPa	4.67	5.01

a) What does this result suggest about the cause of cyanosis?

....

....

....

....

EXAM 1 : CASE HISTORIES

Case History 1

a) Colonoscopy and biopsy
b) Crohn's disease

Discussion

Crohn's disease has recently increased in incidence to about 5 per 100,000, equal to ulcerative colitis.

Whilst classical presentations are well known, several more unusual presentations are described. Anorexia nervosa is characteristically associated with an abnormal body image which is unlikely in Crohn's disease.

As it affects the entire GI tract, cheilitis is important to note as is the characteristic full upper lip of aphthous ulceration. The diagnosis has even been made following upper GI endoscopy revealing aphthous ulceration in the oesophagus.

In diagnosis, ESR or more specifically C-reactive protein and orosomucoid may be raised; barium meal and follow through would also be an acceptable answer.

Case History 2

a) Organic and amino acid screen
b) Inborn error of metabolism

Key Points

- Early presentation.
- Vomiting after milk feeds.
- Severe metabolic acidosis.
- The CSF results are normal for a neonate.
- Prematurity is not relevant to the answer.
- The cerebral ultrasound appearance is of non-specific cerebral oedema reflecting the effect of acidosis.
- No more specific wording than inborn error of metabolism is required as the final answer.

Discussion

Although the range of possible symptoms in babies with metabolic errors is wide, two frequent patterns exist. The first pattern begins with vomiting, acidosis and cirulatory disturbance, followed by depressed consciousness and convulsions. This is suggestive of the organic acidaemias.

The second pattern is dominated by neurological features with lethargy, refusal to feed, drowsiness, unconsciousness and convulsions. Hypotonia may be a marked feature. Primary defects of the urea cycle and disorders such as glycine encephalopathy and β-alaninaemia should then be considered.

Answers mentioning sepsis and blood cultures would also score some marks. Alternative investigations are blood glucose, calcium and drug screen.

Case History 3

a) Paired acute and convalescent serum titres for mycoplasma
    Blood cultures
    Immunofluorescent staining of the sputum
b) Oral erythromycin

Key Points
- Dry cough.
- Systemic illness.
- Headaches.
- An important clue is that the illness has not responded to first line antibiotics.

Discussion

This is a typical history for an atypical pneumonia. Note also the anaemia and reticulocytosis suggesting cold agglutinins directed against red cells. The budgerigar (but not the cat) would be a relevant vector for *Chlamydia psittaci*. Note that whilst *Mycoplasma pneumoniae* may produce any X-ray appearance including lobar consolidation, *C. psittaci* generally produces bilateral patchy consolidation. Blood cultures are positive in less than 25% of community acquired pneumonias. Antibody titres are the main diagnostic tests available for atypical pneumonias. Mycoplasma specific IgM is a useful early test but not widely available.

Case History 4

a) Inhalation of foreign body with supervening chest infection
b) Bronchoscopy

Key Points
- The blow to the chest is irrelevant.
- 'Sudden paroxysm of severe coughing' should be enough to raise the possibility of inhalation of a foreign body.

Discussion

Edible nuts make up 50% of intrabronchial foreign bodies. 66% are diagnosed in the first week, others may go unrecognised for months. Most lodge in a main or stem bronchus, right side more often than left. If the clinical and radiological pattern of illness is suggestive, bronchoscopy should be carried out even without a history of inhalation.

Delayed diagnosis may present as
    recurrent wheeze
    persistent chest infection
    chronic cough with haemoptysis
    lung collapse with respiratory failure

Late diagnosis may result in infection distal to the bronchial obstruction. Removal may fail if the foreign body breaks up. On occasion, if removal fails, thoracotomy and resection may be required. Follow up after successful removal should be by ventilation perfusion lung scan, a more sensitive index of lung damage than chest X-ray in this case. Ventilation-perfusion scan will show a persistent abnormality if the foreign body has been in situ for more than 24 hours.

Case History 5

a) Full blood count and film
b) Blood pressure and weight
c) Haemolytic uraemic syndrome

Key Points

- Haemolytic uraemic syndrome (H.U.S.) now affects 150 children a year in the U.K. and should be considered in any preschool child with bloody diarrhoea.
- Pallor and jaundice in this case reflect haemolysis.
- A blood film will demonstrate anaemia, thrombocytopenia and features of microangiopathic haemolytic anaemia.

Discussion

H.U.S. defines a group of conditions in which microangiopathic haemolytic anaemia coexists with acute renal impairment. It now represents the most common cause of childhood acute renal failure in Europe. Abdominal pain is not uncommon and appendicitis or intussusception may be suspected.

Stool cultures may yield *Escherichia coli* serotype 0157:H7 producing verotoxin. The D+ form with prodromal diarrhoea has a good long term outcome in 80% of cases if dialysis is avoided. The less common D- form, which may be familial or relapsing, carries a poor prognosis.

EXAM 1 : DATA INTERPRETATIONS

Question 1

a) Sickle cell beta + thalassaemia
b) Beta + thalassaemia

Discussion

Haemoglobin	*Structure*	*Comment*
A	$\alpha 2\beta 2$	92% of all adult Hb
A2	$\alpha 2\delta 2$	2% of adult Hb elevated in β thal
F	$\alpha 2\gamma 2$	normal haemoglobin in fetus stays elevated in β thal
Barts	$\beta 4$	Found in α thal. Biologically useless
H	$\gamma 4$	100% of haemoglobin in homozygous α thal, biologically useless

Electrophoresis

Sickle cell disease	HbS, no HbA HbF variable 5-15%
Sickle trait	HbS 25-45% HbA
β-Thal trait	HbA HbA2 >3.5% makes the diagnosis ± HbF
β-Thal major	HbA virtually absent HbF majority HbA2 variable low/normal/raised
Sickle thalassaemia	HbS HbF ±HbA

Clinical and haematological manifestations of sickle thalassaemia are variable, much of this due to two types of abnormal beta chain synthesis. β° denotes no beta chain production. β^{+} small amounts beta chain synthesis.

Patients with sickle thalassaemia in general do not require blood transfusions, but many suffer severe sickle-cell crises.

Question 2

a) X linked hypophosphataemic rickets

Type	Ca	PO$_4$	AKP	PTH	25(OH)D3	1,25 (OH)D3	AA-uria
D defct	↓/N	↓/N	↑	↑	↓	↓/N	+
D dep 1	↓	↓/N	↑ ↑	↑	N	↓ ↓	+ +
D dep 2	↓	↓/N	↑ ↑	↑	N	↑ ↑	+
X linked	N	↓ ↓	↑	N	N	N/↓	-

D defct = Vitamin D deficient
D dep 1 = Vitamin D dependent type 1
D dep 2 = Vitamin D dependent type 2
X linked = Familial, X-linked hypophosphataemic rickets

Question 3

a) X-linked dominant.
    This is a better answer than simple autosomal dominant.
    Note absence of transmission from male to male.

Question 4

a) A normal EEG

Discussion

EEGs are common data questions. They are not complicated and simply a matter of pattern recognition. You will need to know about seven 'patterns' as well as the normal trace. Here is a simple guide:

1. Read the question, noting the age and drug treatment.

2. Check the time marker. This is usually at the top of the EEG in 1 second intervals and allows calculation of the frequency of any complex.

3. Check the amplitude scale.

4. Check the montage (map). This is basically a pictorial representation of the sites between which a potential difference is being measured.

5. Now look at the traces:
   What is its nature — spike/sharp wave, slow wave, complex
   Is it present in all channels (generalised)
   Is it in one area only (focal)

6. Is there a pattern?
   3 per second spike wave in absences
   Periodic complexes — SSPE/Herpes simplex encephalitis
   Chaotic large voltage complex — Hypsarrhythmia
   Rolandic spikes etc

Normal EEGs
In young or premature babies there is little difference between the sleeping and waking state. Electrical activity is irregular and intermittent so interpretation requires a great deal of skill. With increasing maturity the cerebral potentials become rhythmic and a dominant rhythm emerges, initially slow 4 to 6 Hz becoming faster to form the alpha rhythm 8 to 12 Hz characteristic of the adult EEG. This EEG shows 8 to 12 Hz alpha waves, amplitudes less than $50\,\mu$V.

Question 5

a) Cystic fibrosis
b) Hyponatraemia, hypokalaemic metabolic alkalosis
c) Pseudo-Bartter's syndrome secondary to hyperaldosteronism in cystic fibrosis

Discussion

Sweat test
a) 100 mg of sweat is the minimum that should be collected for a test to be valid.
b) Normal children aged between 4 weeks and 13 years have Na < 60 mmol and Cl < 50 mmol/l.
c) The test is consistent with cystic fibrosis if Na > 60 and Cl > 70 mmol/l.

The electrolyte pattern is termed pseudo-Bartter's, producing the same hypokalaemic alkalosis as seen in Bartter's syndrome, with hyperplasia of the juxtaglomerular apparatus. There is persistent hyponatraemia and hypokalaemia secondary to excessive sweat electrolyte loss. These children need large quantities of supplemental sodium and potassium during the first few months of life.

Question 6

a) Restrictive
b) Myasthenia gravis
   Fibrosing alveolitis
   Scoliosis

Discussion

Forced vital capacity is the total volume of gas expelled during forced expiration. This volume is reduced in conditions with reduced pulmonary compliance (stiff lungs), reduced lung volume or neuromuscular disease. The volume of this gas expired within the first second is the FEV_1. This is also reduced in restrictive lung disease but proportionately to the total lung volume. As a result, FEV_1/FVC is normal in restrictive lung disease.

Question 7

a) One and a half years.

Question 8

a) Ventricular septal defect; right ventricular outflow tract obstruction
b) Fallot's tetralogy

Cardiac catheter data are best interpreted by following saturation and then pressure measurements through each chamber in anatomical sequence from systemic venous to systemic arterial. It may be simpler to draw a diagram listing the abnormalities (see normal values).

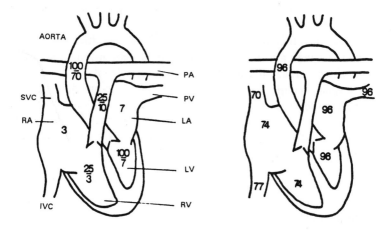

normal pressure measurements (mmHg)   normal oxygen saturation (%)

There is a step-up in oxygen saturation between right atrium and right ventricle implying a left to right shunt at ventricular level.

The pressure gradient between the right ventricle and pulmonary artery implies right ventricular outflow tract obstruction.

These features, in addition to desaturation seen in the aorta suggest the diagnosis of Fallot's tetralogy.

Question 9

a) Conductive hearing loss
b) Serous otitis media

Discussion

Measurement of the thresholds for air and bone conduction are usually obtained by pure tone audiometry. Stimuli of different frequencies ranging from 250 to 8,000 Hz are emitted at different intensities above the threshold of normal hearing.

Key Points

- A sound made through a headphone of a standard audiometer will also be heard in the contralateral ear if the source in that ear is 50 dB or greater. At this stage, masking of the non-test ear has to be undertaken.

- For bone conduction testing when the vibrator is placed on the skull, there is virtually no loss of sound heard in the non-test ear, thus masking should always be undertaken.

In this example there is a wide threshold between air conduction and bone conduction, an 'air-bone gap'. This implies the hearing loss is due to a malfunction of the conducting system of the external and middle ear, rather than a sensori-neural mechanism.

Conductive deafness is the most common type of hearing loss in children. It may be due to secretory otitis media, acute otitis media or congenital abnormalities of the external or middle ear.

Intermittent conductive deafness, provided speech and language are not delayed, is reviewed with audiograms and tympanometry and may resolve spontaneously.

Persistent hearing loss due to middle ear fluid is an indication for referral to an ENT surgeon for possible myringotomy/grommets or adenoidectomy.

Question 10

a) Septic screen including lumbar puncture
b) Congenital adrenal hypoplasia
c) Salt, hydrocortisone and fludrocortisone

This is a sick male infant who on admission has lost more than 10% of his bodyweight and is passing a dilute urine with inappropriately high sodium content. Obviously sepsis needs to be excluded and overwhelming urinary tract infection occasionally mimics this picture.

Congenital adrenal hyperplasia should be the working clinical diagnosis once sepsis is ruled out. However, the results show that 17-hydroxy-progesterone is low and distal metabolites are also low (see steroid synthesis pathway). Congenital adrenal hypoplasia is less common than hyperplasia which itself is rare. 21-hydroxylase deficiency is the most common variety.

EXAM 2 : CASE HISTORIES

Case History 1

a) Accidental drug ingestion, phenothiazine group
b) Good prognosis if supportive management of airway, breathing and circulation is satisfactory

Key Points

- Oculogyric crises in children are most commonly the result of drug ingestion.
- Look for clues in the history such as recent bereavement, schizophrenia, travel sickness etc.
- Learn normal values for CSF; note the different ranges for neonates and older children. This result is normal.

Discussion

Overdosage with phenothiazines causes hypotension, hypothermia, cardiac arrythmias, convulsions and extrapyramidal reactions. Treatment is supportive and symptomatic. Dystonic reactions may be treated with benztropine or procyclidine injection. Diazepam may be used to control convulsions.

Case History 2

a) Pericardial aspiration and biopsy with staining and culture for T.B.
   Echocardiography
b) Tuberculous constrictive pericarditis

Key Point
- Asian origin and long history of malaise should alert one to the possibility of T.B.

Several vital clinical points

It is unusual not to be able to palpate the apex beat in a thin boy. The JVP is raised and there is hepatomegaly, ascites (transudate) out of proportion to the signs and symptoms of heart disease. Mantoux test may be negative in severe active T.B. It may be positive if 1:1,000 strength used.

Discussion

Constrictive pericarditis is caused by a wide variety of diseases, most cases probably originating as pericardial inflammation with effusion. The pericardium may become thick, fibrous and calcified, impeding cardiac filling.

Chest X-ray may show a small heart and calcification on lateral views, or be normal as in this example. ECG characteristically shows low voltage QRS complexes and T wave inversion. The echocardiogram may demonstrate thickened pericardium and abnormal motion of the ventricular septum and posterior left ventricular wall.

Standard antituberculous chemotherapy (rifampicin, isoniazid and pyrazinamide for 2 months then rifampicin and isoniazid for 4 months). An eleven week course of prednisolone is advised and surgical removal of a substantial proportion of the pericardium is required. Pyridoxine should be taken during antituberculous therapy.

Case History 3

a) Renal vein thrombosis
b) Renal ultrasound scan
   Blood culture and sensitivity
   Serum creatinine
c) Hypernatraemia
   Intracranial haemorrhage
   Hypertension

Key Points
- The age group, preceding diarrhoea and palpable kidney make the diagnosis of renal vein thrombosis likely.
- Thrombocytopenia and uraemia make this even more likely.
- It is reasonable to ask for serum creatinine as this is not given in the question.

Discussion

One third of all cases of renal vein thrombosis are detected in the first week of life. Severity varies from grave bilateral involvement to focal involvement of one kidney. Asphyxia, prematurity, dehydration, sepsis and maternal diabetes are possible predisposing factors. In severe cases, peritoneal dialysis and intensive care on a paediatric nephrology unit is indicated. Careful follow-up is required as the affected kidney may cause severe hypertension via a renin mediated pathway and should in that case be removed.

Case History 4

a) Severe combined immunodeficiency
b) *Pneumocystis carinii*
c) High dose intravenous co-trimoxazole

Key Point
- Early death in a first degree relative should arouse suspicion of recessively inherited disorders.

Discussion

This is a familial immune deficiency with early onset. There is panhypogammaglobulinaemia with low normal white count and absent lymphadenopathy in the presence of diarrhoea and pneumonia. No differential count is given but excluding eosinophils the white count is 3.3.

Agammaglobulinaemia alone presents usually at 4 to 6 months when maternally transferred antibodies are exhausted, diarrhoea also is not a common presenting feature. Thus a combined humoral and cellular deficiency exists.

Wiskott-Aldrich is a possibility but usually is associated with thrombocytopenia, increased IgA, normal IgG and half normal IgM levels. SCID has many familial forms in both autosomal and sex linked recessive forms. The skin rash may be chronic candida.

Functional antibodies such as isohaemagglutinins will be absent and there will be absent sensitivity to candida skin testing. Chronic rotavirus carriage is common. Purine nucleoside phosphorylase or adenosine deaminase levels may be diminished in the parents.

Management is supportive until a histocompatible bone marrow donor becomes available. Blood transfusions should be irradiated to reduce the risk of graft versus host reaction.

Case History 5

a) Ketotic hypoglycaemia
b) Carefully controlled provocation fast

Key Points
- Note the low birth weight, neuroglycopenic symptoms of ataxia and irritability after overnight fast.
- Fasting glucose is well below normal values.
- Phenobarbitone has been started for the hypoglycaemic fits and does not necessarily imply that the child has idiopathic epilepsy.

Discussion

Ketotic hypoglycaemia is the most common cause of hypoglycaemia and presents usually between 1 and 5 years of age. Affected children (usually boys, M:F 2:1) are small and thin. The basic biochemical defect is unknown but hepatic glycogen is known to be depleted and it is postulated that there is a failure in mobilisation of amino acids from muscle for gluconeogenesis in starvation. Due to accelerated starvation, free fatty acid oxidation is increased giving the disorder its name.

The diagnosis is established by excluding metabolic errors and hormone deficiencies. Either with a carefully supervised provocative fast or prior to a spontaneous episode of hypoglycaemia, urine will become ketotic prior to hypoglycaemia and serial blood glucose should demonstrate impending hypoglycaemia within 8 to 16 hours (24 to 36 in normal children). Simultaneous measurements should be as follows:

Insulin	low
GH	elevated
Cortisol	elevated
Thyroxine	normal
Free fatty acids	elevated
Beta hydroxybutyrate	elevated
Ketones	elevated
Amino acids	decreased alanine
Urine	
Reducing substances	negative

Ketones marked	positive
Organic acids	elevated ketones only

In patients with ketotic hypoglycaemia, there is no response to glucagon in the fasted state but a response is present in the fed state. Glucagon stimulation test should not be necessary if the provocation test is successful.

During a hypoglycaemic attack the child should be given glucose in its most convenient form. Children do well with frequent high protein, high carbohydrate meals (4 or 5 a day). During periods of illness or fasting, high carbohydrate drinks should be offered at frequent intervals. Spontaneous remission occurs by 9 to 10 years.

EXAM 2 : DATA INTERPRETATION PAPER

Question 1

a) Nephrotic syndrome due to minimal change nephritis
b) 24 hour urine protein/creatinine estimation
   Complement levels
   Blood pressure
   Serum (creatinine)
c) Careful fluid management
   Prednisolone 60 mg/m^2 until urine protein free, then 40 mg/m^2 for a month
   Penicillin

Minimal change nephritis is the most common pathology underlying childhood nephrotic syndrome. There is an increased incidence amongst the Asian population. Complement level is normal in minimal change but low in more serious renal disease such as SLE, post-streptococcal nephritis, SBE, cryoglobulinaemia and mesangiocapillary glomerulonephritis.

Question 2

a) Primary generalised non-convulsant epilepsy (Childhood absence)
b) Hyperventilation
c) No

Discussion

Childhood absence epilepsy

Clinical characteristics
a) Age at onset 3-13 years
b) Normal neurological examination and intelligence
c) Seizures are typical absences (simple or complex) at onset, followed or not by generalised tonic-clonic seizures

EEG features
a) Background is normal
b) Ictal shows bilateral, synchronous, symmetrical spike waves, usually at 3 Hz spontaneously and/or activated by hyperventilation

If these criteria are satisfied further neuroimaging is not necessary prior to treatment with either ethosuximide or sodium valproate.

Question 3

a) 50% of boys will have a low G6PD
b) 50% of girls will have a marginally low G6PD

The G6PD enzyme is on the X chromosome. G6PD is the rate limiting enzyme of the pentose phosphate pathway and so important for protecting the red cell from oxidant stress. More than 100 distinct enzyme variants of G6PD have been documented.

Question 4

a) GH deficiency
   Primary hypothyroidism
   GnRH deficiency

Pituitary damage following cranial irradiation is common, GH deficiency occurring in 97% of cases, with peak incidence 2 years after radiotherapy. This boy, having a medulloblastoma, would also have had spinal irradiation, accounting for thyroid damage as reflected in the high TSH levels. This occurs in about 30% of cases. GnRH deficiency is less common.

Question 5

a) Acquired Immune Deficiency Syndrome (AIDS)
b) Polymerase chain amplification of HIV nucleic acid
   cd4:cd8 ratio

Discussion

Materno-fetal transmission is responsible for 80% of paediatric HIV infection in the U.K. With routine screening of blood products, the number of children infected through transfusion of blood or products has been minimised.

The vertical transmission risk in Europe is about 13% (i.e. the risk of the child being HIV antibody positive at 18 months); the risk is higher in Africa for various reasons.

Clinical features
Presenting symptoms — 75% are non-specific, including
   failure to thrive
   recurrent bacterial infections
   chronic diarrhoea
   skin infections
there may also be hepatosplenomegaly and lymphadenopathy

Neurodevelopment
    developmental delay
    regression of developmental milestones
    acquired microcephaly
    gait abnormalities

Pulmonary disease
    Pneumocystis carinii pneumonia
    lymphoid interstitial pneumonitis

Secondary infection
    recurrent infection of respiratory tract with encapsulated organisms
    (*Pneumocystis, Haemophilus*)
    recurrent meningitis; abscesses

Diagnosis
Before 18 months when HIV antibody may still be passively acquired:
a) Polymerase chain reaction, amplifies extremely small amounts of host nucleic acid to detectable levels. This forms the basis of a very sensitive test which will detect a single molecule of viral nucleic acid amongst the DNA of a host cell.
b) Polyclonal hypergammaglobulinaemia. This has been shown to be sensitive and specific as early as 3 months.
c) Low cd4:cd8 ratio. Specific but not as sensitive as hypergammaglobulinaemia.
d) Clinical criteria. In the early stages these are probably the least sensitive and specific.

Treatment
Trials currently underway using AZT and intravenous immunoglobulin therapy. Little information at present about correct doses or frequency of AZT in children. In adults AZT has not been shown to alter the rates of seroconversion.

Question 6

a) Long PR interval
    Superior axis
    Neonatal RS progression
b) Atrioventricular septal defect

Question 7

1493 N

a) Unilateral high voltage centrotemporal spikes
b) Benign childhood epilepsy or benign rolandic epilepsy

Discussion

This condition accounts for about 16% of childhood epilepsy. The family history of epilepsy in first degree relatives is positive in about 30%. Seizures may be simple partial, especially in daytime, or generalised tonic-clonic, especially in sleep.

Treatment depends on the number of seizures as with or without treatment spontaneous remission typically occurs before the age of 15 years and outlook for future scholastic achievement is good.

EEG

Background is normal
Interictal shows unilateral and/or bilateral blunt high amplitude centrotemporal spikes.

Question 8

a) Partially treated bacterial meningitis

Typical CSF findings after 1st year of life:

Diagnosis	Cells/mm³	Protein g/l	Glucose mmol/l
Normal	0-5, lymphocytes	0.2-0.4	2.8-4.8
Bacterial	200-2,000 (PMN)	Increased	very low
Viral	100-1,000 (lymphocytes)	N/↑ 0.45-0.85	N (↓ in mumps)
TB	100-1,000 (lymphocytes)	↑ 0.6-5.0	↓ 0.5-2.0

Question 9

a) Increase the I:E ratio
   Increase the Peak Airway Pressure

These two manoeuvres increase the mean airway pressure.

Question 10

a) Distal renal tubular acidosis (type I)
b) Hereditary
   Idiopathic
   Ehlers Danlos
   Amphotericin
   Hypercalcaemia
   Hypokalaemia
c) Shohl's solution — potassium and sodium citrate
   Nephrolithotomy

This is a hyperchloraemic (normal anion gap) acidosis with hypokalaemia. Renal tubular acidosis is caused by abnormalities in renal regulation of bicarbonate. Patients with this type of RTA may present with unexplained acidosis, failure to thrive, hypokalaemia, or one of the complications such as nephrolithiasis, nephrocalcinosis, rickets or polyuria. The urine pH does not fall below 6. Hypokalaemia is common and may be severe. Hypercalciuria is common and urinary citrate excretion is low.

Administration of alkali in the form of sodium bicarbonate or sodium citrate, the latter usually given as Shohl's solution which contains 1 mmol of citrate per ml of solution. A proportion of the alkali can be given as potassium bicarbonate or citrate.

EXAM 3 : CASE HISTORIES

Case History 1

a) Acute lymphoblastic leukaemia
b) Bone marrow biopsy
   Peripheral blood film

Key Points
- A multisystem disease with several features in the history:
  - a) Bleeding disorder — unexplained bruise
  - b) Fever and sore throat
  - c) Painless lymphadenopathy
  - d) Spinal cord lesion in the lumbar region
  - e) Possible meningitis — stiff neck and back
- Acute lymphoblastic leukaemia with meningeal infiltration is the most likely explanation.

Discussion

Acute leukaemia is the commonest malignant condition of childhood, the leukaemias together accounting for 30% of childhood cancers.
About 70% are acute lymphoblastic (ALL), 20% acute myeloblastic (AML) or variants.

Prognosis
ALL generally better than AML
Common and T cell better than B cell
High WBC > 60,000 carries poor prognosis
Age at presentation < 1 year or > 14 years poor prognosis
Presence of CNS involvement at diagnosis is an unfavourable feature
Prognosis is better if remission achieved within 14 days of induction

Overall survival 75%.

Case History 2

a) Blocked endotracheal tube
   Displaced endotracheal tube
   Pneumothorax requiring drainage
   Ventilator failure

Key Points

- This question aims to establish whether the candidate has practical experience of working in a neonatal unit.
- The question is quite specific in describing a rapidly correctable situation and so intraventricular haemorrhage and sepsis would be incorrect answers.
- As neonatology achieves a higher profile in paediatrics, so the number of questions devoted to neonatology will increase.

Case History 3

a) Visit to a forest or foreign land
b) Serum specific IgM to *Borrelia burgdorferi*
c) Penicillin; tetracycline is contraindicated because of the effect on growing teeth

Erythema chronicum migrans, the most common manifestation of Lyme disease, begins usually 4 to 20 days after the bite of an *ixodid* tick. An erythematous macule forms gradually enlarging to form a plaque-like, erythematous annular lesion of median diameter 16 cm. The usual sites include the thigh, buttocks and axillae. Half the patients have multiple secondary annular lesions. The average duration of the untreated lesion is 3 weeks. The rash may be confused with streptococcal cellulitis, erythema muliforme (when multiple) or erythema marginatum. Often, ECM is associated with systemic symptoms such as malaise, fatigue, headache, stiff neck, and arthralgia. Fever is usually low grade but may be as high as 40°C. Regional lymphadenopathy, anicteric hepatitis, conjunctivitis or pharyngitis may also occur. These symptoms usually resolve over several days but may be intermittent over several weeks.

Neurological involvement usually occurs within four weeks of the tick bite. Meningitis, cranial nerve palsies and peripheral neuropathy are most common, whilst meningoencephalitis, Guillain-Barré syndrome, pseudotumour cerebri and myelitis may also occur. Cardiac abnormalities occur more commonly in young adult males. Arthritis has been described in the U.S.A. but rarely in the U.K.

The diagnosis is made on clinical and epidemiological grounds and confirmed by specific serology. The organism may be isolated from blood or cerebrospinal fluid.

Case History 4

a) Meconium ileus equivalent
   Intussusception
   Appendix abscess
b) Gastrografin enema

Discussion

Meconium ileus can produce intestinal obstruction in cystic fibrosis at any time from neonatal (or uterine) to adult life. In the initial stages either 50 ml oral gastrografin or acetylcysteine 5 ml tds may relieve the obstruction. A gastrografin enema, provided the patient is stable with no signs of perforation or dehydration, can be both diagnostic and therapeutic.

Where presumptive cases of meconium ileus equivalent fail to respond to the above measures, intussusception must be considered and surgery may be necessary.

Case History 5

a) Guillain-Barré syndrome/Ascending polyneuritis
b) Lumbar puncture
c) Serial vital capacity

Key Points
- The past history of meningitis is irrelevant.
- Expressionless face is a clue to facial weakness.
- Be precise in answering the question.

Discussion

A three day history of limb weakness, facial weakness and double vision with absent peripheral reflexes. The imminent danger is of respiratory muscle involvement with consequent respiratory failure.

Lumbar puncture may show cyto-albumin dissociation. Nerve conduction studies are of assistance in making the diagnosis at an early stage. The differential diagnosis here would be myasthenia gravis.

EXAM 3 : DATA INTERPRETATION PAPER

Question 1

a) Pyloric stenosis causing hypochloraemic alkalosis

Question 2

a) 1 in 50,000
b) Less than 1%

Four fifths of achondroplastics are new genetic mutations, born to unaffected parents. Although neither parent is affected, the risk of having another affected child is above that of the general population as one of the parents may exhibit gonadal mosaicism.

Question 3

a) Nesidioblastosis

Note the markedly elevated and inappropriate insulin level and absence of ketones. Hypoglycaemia may usefully be considered in terms of the presence or absence of ketonuria. The former implies a lack of substrate and the latter a hyperinsulinaemic state.

Nesidioblastosis is the most common hyperinsulinaemic state and presents usually in the first weeks or months of life. There is disordered islet cell organisation and a relative somatostatin deficiency allowing an inappropriate rise in insulin levels (normal $\leq$ 10 mU/l when blood glucose < 2.5 mmol/l).

Hypoglycaemia in hyperinsulinism may require intravenous dextrose infusion at rates up to 20 mg/kg/min. There is no response to glucagon. Diazoxide inhibits insulin secretion and subtotal pancreatectomy may be required if this fails.

Question 4

a) Obstructive airways disease
   Increased residual volume
   Reversibility
b) Whole body plethysmography
   Helium dilution

Discussion

Obstructive lung disease is often defined as reversible if, following administration of a bronchodilator, there is a 15% improvement in FEV_1. Airways disease accelerates the increase in residual volume. Any airways narrowing or loss of recoil, allowing dynamic compression, facilitates air trapping within the lungs and hence an increased residual volume is a characteristic feature of obstructive airways disease.

The total lung capacity depends on the balance of the ability of the respiratory muscles to expand the chest and the tendency of the lungs and chest wall to recoil inward towards their resting position. The increase in lung disease is due primarily to the loss of elastic recoil, often related to localised damage with lung cysts or bullae.

Question 5

a) Karyotype
   Thyroid function tests
b) Primary hypothyroidism
c) Thyroxine replacement therapy, a marked personality change may occur in the child.

Delayed bone age and declining height velocity are firm reasons to investigate this girl's short stature. Turner's syndrome and hypothyroidism should be considered in any teenage girl who presents in this way, even if the clinical features are not obvious.

In a standard insulin tolerance test there should be an appropriate hypoglycaemia, GH should rise to exceed 12.5, cortisol should double its base level. FSH/LH should rise in parallel to GnRH challenge. In this example, the GH response is boderline low but the most striking abnormality is the very high baseline TSH which is unresponsive to TRH implying that this is primary organ associated hypothyroidism.

Thyroxine replacement therapy should be commenced with great care because of its effects on the cardiovascular system. Progress should be monitored symptomatically and by the TSH level. Parents should be warned that a previously inactive docile child will become more energetic and her school performance may also suffer until stabilisation is attained.

Question 6

a) Complete atrio ventricular conduction block (heart block)

Question 7

a) Leukaemia
   Systemic lupus erythematosus

Pancytopenia with haematuria may be due to marrow replacement or suppression. Nephritis may also be present in SLE. Aplastic anaemia is another possible answer.

Question 8

a) Kawasaki disease
b) Echocardiogram
c) Intravenous gammaglobulin 400 mg/kg/d and oral aspirin, high dose until fever settles then low dose thereafter.

Criteria for diagnosis:

1) Persistent high fever for at least five days
2) Bilateral conjunctival injection
3) Pleomorphic rash
4) Swelling and induration of hands and feet
5) Desquamation of fingers and toes
6) Cervical lymphadenopathy

Strict case definition requires the presence of at least five of the six criteria, or of four plus coronary artery aneurysms. With the help of echo-cardiography however, Kawasaki disease is being diagnosed increasingly often in patients with three or fewer of the major signs.

Question 9

a) Four and a half years
b) Formal test of hearing

Discussion

Shapes
Children can imitate before they can copy a shape, so read the question carefully. From three years children are generally asked to copy shapes.

	50th centile	90th centile
Vertical line	2½ years	3 years
Circle	2 years 9 months	3 ½ years
Cross	4 years	4 years 8 months
Square	4 years 7 months	5 years 3 months
Triangle	5 years	5 ½ years

Hearing and language
At 4 years most children can count to ten without a mistake. By 3 years 5 months 90% of children can give their first and family name. Failure in these aspects may represent developmental delay or psychosocial deprivation. The most important initial step is to test this child's hearing formally. A speech discrimination test would be useful as an initial screen, although free field audiometry would be more precise.

Question 10

a) Reticulocyte count
   Bone marrow examination
   Blood film
b) Diamond-Blackfan syndrome/Pure red cell aplasia

The baby's anaemia is not due to Rhesus or ABO incompatibility. The white count and platelets are normal. Diamond-Blackfan syndrome usually presents with profound anaemia by 2 to 6 months. The most important diagnostic feature is the absence of red cell precursors in blood and bone marrow. Erythropoietin levels are high.

Treatment is supportive with transfusions and steroids. A few cases remit spontaneously, otherwise death occurs in the second decade without bone marrow transplantation.

EXAM 4 : CASE HISTORIES

Case History 1

a) Pulmonary hypertension
b) Atrial fibrillation
c) Pulmonary embolism

A loud second (presumed pulmonary) heart sound accompanied by diastolic murmur signifies pulmonary hypertension with functional valvular incompetence. This is a serious complication of a systemic-pulmonary shunt. Pulmonary embolism is a well know consequence of atrial fibrillation. Endocarditis should be borne in mind in questions of this nature. Patch detachment is an early complication.

Case History 2

a) Septic screen including lumbar puncture
    Blood glucose
    Serum calcium and electrolytes
b) Drug withdrawal

Key Points

- Several classical features of withdrawal — jitteriness, temperature instability, sweatiness, tachycardia. Feeding disturbance such as increased demand and disordered suck occurs.
- In this case the feeding history makes severe sepsis unlikely.
- Note also the unbooked pregnancy and the absence of antenatal information.

Discussion

Drug withdrawal is increasingly commonly seen. Symptoms also include diarrhoea, rhinorrhoea, apnoea and convulsions and may start at any time in the first two weeks. Methadone, a heroin substitute, causes a period of withdrawal lasting up to three months. Withdrawal can be suppressed with chlorpromazine or diazepam (small doses of morphine in U.S.A.) reducing over several weeks. Drug abuse in the mother should prompt investigation of the social situation and exclusion of HIV and Hepatitis B.

Case History 3

a) ASOT 1,200 I.U.
b) Sydenham's chorea
c) Penicillin
d) Usually normal

Key Points
- The abnormal movements described are choreiform. The possible differential is stereotypy which consists of the same movement repeated, usually sparing the face.
- Absence of a family history or drug ingestion (neuroleptics, phenytoin).
- The story of a fright is irrelevant and the 'old council house' is a false clue for lead poisoning.

Discussion

The onset of Sydenham's chorea is usually insidious, more common in girls with fidgetiness, frowning, head and eye rolling, slurred speech, jerky respiration and exaggerated incoordinated movements. All abnormal movements are made worse by excitement and cease in sleep. Mental state may be labile. Cardiac disease may be present but usually there is no fever or signs of rheumatic fever.

Investigations aim to prove the presence of streptococcal infection and search for other organ damage.

Treatment traditionally includes bed rest, a course of penicillin and prophylaxis until adult life, psychological and physiotherapy support, and follow up, if appropriate, for cardiac disease.

Case History 4

a) Thyroid function tests
b) Untreated at 10 weeks
   Both parents of low intelligence

Congenital hypothyroidism has an incidence of 1 in 3,000, three times as common in girls as in boys. It has recently been demonstrated that thyroid hormones can cross the placenta, hence infants are not frankly 'cretinous' at birth. It is possible that one or both parents are also affected. Hirschsprung's is associated. Feeding difficulties and nasal obstruction are typical. The temperature is subnormal and anaemia refractory to haematinics occurs.

Below are clinical features described in congenital hypothyroidism*. Since the early signs are generally non-specific and the development of other features is slow, thyroid function tests should be performed in case of doubt.

Features which may be present at birth
Postmature, large size
Wide posterior fontanelle
Umbilical hernia
Goitre

Early signs, less than four weeks
Placid, 'good', sleeps a lot
Poor feeder
Constipation, abdominal distension
Mottled, cold
Oedema
Prolonged jaundice

Late signs
Cretinous appearance
Big tongue
Hoarse cry
Dry skin and hair
Slow responses
Retarded growth and development

(*Taken from Roberton N.R.C. A Textbook of Neonatology. Churchill Livingstone)

The age at treatment and the genetic potential endowed by the parents limit the mental development. Patients in whom treatment is started before 6 weeks of age have an average IQ of 100. If treatment is started between 6 weeks and 3 months IQ drops to 95; between 3 and 6 months to 75; after 6 months, 55 or less.

Several other neurological deficits have been described including deafness, ataxia, attention deficit disorder, abnormal muscle tone and speech defects.

This question is a bit old fashioned as most children would be expected to have been detected at neonatal screening.

Case History 5

a) Coeliac disease
b) Jejunal biopsy for histological diagnosis

Key Points
- It is important not to be distracted by issues such as congenital heart disease or drug therapeutics.
- Congenital heart disease is responsible for poor growth in some circumstances, digoxin overdose may cause nausea and vomiting but the question asks for the *most likely* cause.
- Contained in this question is a classical description of a child presenting with coeliac disease.

Discussion

Coeliac disease is a gluten induced enteropathy requiring characteristic histological findings to confirm the diagnosis. Increasing use is being made of specific antibody tests, IgG and IgA antigliadin and antiendomyseal antibodies. In the future, use of these antibody tests and a good response to a gluten free diet may obviate the need for further challenge biopsy. Transient gluten intolerance is more common under one year of age and a gluten challenge should be conducted after one year on a gluten free diet. Other causes of a similar biopsy appearance of total villous atrophy include giardiasis, post-enteritis enteropathy and tropical sprue.

EXAM 4 : DATA INTERPRETATION PAPER

Question 1

a) Intestinal lymphangiectasia
b) Jejunal biopsy
   Chromium labelled albumin studies

Discussion

There are a number of mechanisms in protein losing enteropathies.

a) Exudation from ulcerative   e.g. Crohns; U.C.
   or inflammatory lesion   Intestinal T.B.

b) Defective lymphatic   e.g. Intestinal lymphangiectasia;
   drainage   neoplasia affecting mesenteric
                                   lymphatics

c) Unknown   e.g. Coeliac disease;
                                   Henoch-Schönlein purpura

The diagnosis is made by first excluding cirrhosis and nephrotic syndrome. Confirmation is by demonstrating excess faecal loss of ^{51}Cr labelled albumin. In this particular case the history and investigations suggest a specific diagnosis. Intestinal lymphangiectasia presents in childhood, oedema usually preceding diarrhoea. The characteristic lesion seen on biopsy is dilatation of the small bowel lymphatics. There is always a marked hypoalbuminaemia and all immunoglobulins also reduced. The peripheral white count is always abnormal with a severe reduction of lymphocytes. Treatment is generally supportive with medium chain triglycerides which are more easily absorbed than normal dietary fat.

Question 2

a) X linked recessive
b) Nil
c) 1 in 4

Question 3

a) Encephalitis
b) Herpes simplex virus

Question 4

a) Inorganic lead encephalopathy
b) Free red cell protoporphyrin
   Urine coproporphyrin
   Blood (lead)

There are signs of encephalopathy, anaemia, proteinuria and glycosuria. Lead causes proximal renal tubular damage and by interfering with iron utilisation and haemoglobin synthesis causes hypochromic, microcytic anaemia.

Question 5

a) Profound bilateral sensori-neural hearing loss
b) *Haemophilus influenzae* meningitis

This severe deafness may be caused by meningitis, particularly *H. influenzae*. The chances of this happening in the future are now reduced by the use of dexamethasone in the acute stages of the disease and the new HiB vaccination programme given at 2, 3 and 4 months.

Note also that:

- Only unmasked bone conduction is obtainable in severe binaural disease.
- The air bone gap at 250 and 500 Hz is false as at these frequencies at levels around 50 dBHL bone conduction thresholds are felt through vibration, 'vibration thresholds'.
- Bone conduction thresholds are only measurable 'down' to 60 dBHL and the presence of a false air-bone gap therefore appears in severe or profound losses.

Question 6

a) Supraventricular tachycardia
b) IV adenosine or DC cardioversion

Childhood SVT is associated with a small risk of death. Infants especially tolerate tachycardia less well than adults as they are more dependent on heart rate for cardiac output and have fewer reserves.

Ventricular tachycardia should be excluded. If the child is sick, the child should have DC cardioversion with full resuscitative facilities at hand. However, if the child is tolerating the tachycardia and it is judged to be a junctional tachycardia, a vagal manoeuvre may be successful. This may comprise immersion of the face in cold water, blowing on the face or unilateral carotid sinus massage.

If vagal manoeuvres fail, intravenous adenosine is the drug of choice. It acts by slowing AV nodal conduction, thus disrupting re-entry circuits. It is effective within 10-15 seconds of administration and has a half-life of the same order. Unlike verapamil it is not negatively inotropic in this form. It has a high safety profile, its main drawback being the fact that 30% of tachycardias will reinitiate.

If adenosine fails, the diagnosis should be reconsidered and if the child is still well, a second line drug such as intravenous fleicanide tried. Otherwise DC cardioversion, initially 1J/kg, with a short acting anaesthetic, is an option.

Question 7

a) Infectious mononucleosis
b) Serology for specific Epstein-Barr IgM antibody

Discussion

Clinical presentation of infectious mononucleosis is variable:

General features:	Fever, lymphadenopathy, pharyngitis, splenomegaly (50%), mild hepatomegaly, jaundice
Cardiac:	Myocarditis, arrhythmias
Neurological:	Aseptic meningitis, cranial nerve palsies, transverse myelitis
Haematological:	Atypical monocytes 5-50% total white cell count, actually transformed T cells
	Auto-immune haemolytic anaemia with cold agglutinins
	Thrombocytopenia

Investigations:

The heterophile antibody test (Paul Bunnell) is occasionally negative in early stages of infectious mononucleosis and may also give false positive results. Specific IgM antibody to EBV indicates a very recent or current infection.

Question 8

a) Commence anticonvulsants
b) Serum calcium, CT brain
   Blood culture
   Urine culture
c) Idiopathic epilepsy
   Febrile convulsions
   Subarachnoid haemorrhage in view of the bloodstained CSF

This infant has had three convulsions in the space of a few hours. This may be the presentation of idiopathic epilepsy or simple febrile convulsions, although it should be noted that she is quite young for the latter. Alternatively, we are not told whether the lumbar puncture was traumatic or not, raising the possibility of an intracranial haemorrhage.

Question 9

a) Coarctation of the aorta
   Ventricular septal defect
   Patent ductus arteriosus

Discussion

Working through each chamber sequentially as previously outlined, there is a significant step-up in saturation at right ventricular level, indicating a left to right shunt. The step down at aortic level confirms a right to left shunt via a patent ductus arteriosus.

The history describes a preductal (infantile) coarctation, in which persistence of the ductus arteriosus is a common feature. The descending aorta receives most of its blood supply from the main pulmonary artery via the ductus arteriosus, while the left ventricle continues to supply the first two or three aortic branches. The pulmonary hypertension initially accompanies a high pulmonary blood flow, but may later reflect increasing pulmonary resistance.

In preductal coarctation, congestive cardiac failure is often precipitated in the earliest days or weeks of life. If possible, the preductal segment is excised and either end-to-end anastomosis or subclavian patch repair performed, followed by surgical closure of the ductus arteriosus.

Question 10

a) Anaemia of prematurity

Discussion

The cause of this anaemia is multifactorial. Following the rise in pO_2 after delivery, erythropoietin levels fall and become undetectable in the plasma for 1 to 2 months. In both full term and premature infants the haemoglobin level falls, and in premature infants may fall to 7-8 g/dl during the second month. The red cell lifespan in premature infants is of the order of two weeks. This fall is mirrored by a reticulocyte count of about 4% at birth which falls to 1-2% during the first month.

Folic acid deficiency and vitamin E deficiency may both play a part in anaemia of prematurity but iron deficiency is not important in the early stage.

In this case the reticulocyte response is satisfactory and the haemoglobin usually begins to rise slowly and transfusion is not required.

EXAM 5 : CASE HISTORIES

Case History 1

a) Biliary colic
b) Abdominal ultrasound

Key Points
- Intermittent pain, commencing after mealtimes suggests biliary colic.
- He is comfortable on examination and the pain is settling. The steady haemoglobin value excludes two important differentials in sickle cell disease:

<u>Hepatic sequestration</u>
occurs in all age groups
abdominal distension with severe hypochondrial pain
rapidly enlarging tense liver

<u>Girdle syndrome</u>
silent distended abdomen
hepatic enlargement common
often bilateral basal lung consolidation

Discussion

30% of children and 70% of adults with sickle cell disease have gallstones. These are often asymptomatic but can cause

    acute cholecystitis
    chronic cholangitis
    biliary colic
    obstruction at the common bile duct
    related acute pancreatitis

As many as 50% of stones may be radiopaque so may be visible on plain abdominal X-ray. Ultrasound of gallbladder or oral cholecystogram are most likely to confirm the diagnosis.
Acute cholecystitis is managed with analgesia, hydration and antibiotics. If recurrent problems occur then elective open or laparoscopic cholecystectomy may be necessary, with careful pre-operative preparation often with exchange transfusion.

Case History 2

a) Full blood count including packed cell volume
   Clotting studies
b) Fresh frozen plasma

Key Points

- There is no record that this baby received Vitamin K after birth and this was probably missed in the ambulance and forgotten after admission.
- The sticky stools suggest gastrointestinal haemorrhage.
- Testing the stool for blood is a reasonable answer, but since only two tests are allowed, blood count and clotting are more important.

Discussion

Haemorrhagic disease of the newborn has a significant mortality. Vitamin K even given intravenously does not act immediately and fresh frozen plasma should be given to replace deficient clotting factors.

Following the recent controversy over the link between vitamin K and childhood cancer, it is likely that more cases like this will occur. BPA recommendations suggest three doses of vitamin K orally are as effective as IM treatment, but compliance is then more likely to be a problem.

Case History 3

a) CT brain scan or cerebral angiography
b) Sagittal sinus thrombosis
    Encephalitis or meningitis with raised intracranial pressure

Key Points

- Clinical history of severe dehydration, but a full anterior fontanelle suggests raised intracranial pressure. Normal fundi do not exclude this.
- Note elevated CSF protein value (see normal values).
- The question is specific in asking for investigations to confirm a diagnosis, not immediate investigation, so electrolytes would not be an appropriate answer.

Discussion

Thrombosis of the cerebral veins occurs principally as a complication of severe dehydration, or as an extension of local infection. Sagittal sinus thrombosis occurs mainly in infants who are severely dehydrated often as a consequence of diarrhoea, although one hopes with increasing understanding of oral rehydration therapy it will become less common. The venous obstruction leads to cerebral swelling with signs of raised intracranial pressure including stupor, coma and bulging anterior fontanelle. Seizures and quadraparesis may occur, often with involvement of the extremities first.

Clinically the condition may mimic encephalitis and metabolic encephalopathy. Practically, if there is ever a suspicion of raised intracranial pressure a lumbar puncture should not be performed; normal fundi do not exclude raised intracranial pressure.

A CT scan may show the area of thrombosis, often with widespread haemorrhagic infarction of the brain. Cerebral angiography is of value in localising the site of obstruction. CSF examination is of little help, but pressure is normally elevated, the fluid may be bloody and show white cells and an elevated protein content.

Apart from supportive management, streptokinase infusion may have a role to play although research with this drug has mainly been in adults.

Case History 4

a) Sweat test
   Nasal brushings for ciliary function
   Imunoglobulins
b) Primary ciliary dyskinesia

Key Points
- All the information in this question is relevant, do not miss points like 'thriving'.
- It is important not to dismiss information such as the presence of serous otitis media as a 'red herring', rather consider it in the context of the differential diagnosis.

Discussion

A number of conditions with abnormalities of ciliary function are now recognised.

Kartagener's clasically implies situs inversus, sinusitis and bronchiectasis and is autosomal recessive with incomplete penetrance. Only half of primary ciliary dyskinesia cases have situs inversus.

As the condition is present from birth, these patients have a history of respiratory distress at birth. Later chronic upper and lower respiratory tract disease is almost universal. There is a strong correlation with secretory otitis media and conductive hearing loss.

Diagnosis requires nasal brushings and immediate motility studies by photometric means. Electron microscopy shows a wide variety of structural defects including defective dynein arms or missing spokes.

As the problem is a structural one it is irreversible and so treatment is aimed at delaying onset and progression of bronchiectasis with antibiotics and physiotherapy. Hearing should be tested and ENT intervention sought if appropriate. Many males are infertile and appropriate sperm motility tests and counselling should be carried out.

Case History 5

a) Subdural haematoma
b) Skeletal survey
   CT brain scan
   Clotting studies
c) Liaise with Child Protection Team

Discussion

CT scan adds information about the timing of the haemorrhage. As the haematoma resolves, the appearance of blood changes from a hyperdense to an ultimately hypodense appearance.

A repeated shaking injury can lead to subdural haematoma in the absence of external signs of injury to the head. Cerebral bridging veins are torn at their fixed attachments to sagittal sutures.

The site, age and nature of the haemorrhage all assist in the diagnosis. All children suspected of having intracranial haemorrhage should have a CT scan.

In cases of child abuse, the clinical and pathological features should be viewed in the family context. In determining a course of action, the importance of parental responsibility and the child's own wishes are emphasised in the Children Act.

EXAM 5 : DATA INTERPRETATIONS

Question 1

a) Hypokalaemic alkalosis
b) Urine potassium and chloride
c) Bartter's syndrome

Question 2

a) Autosomal recessive or X-linked recessive
b) Autosomal recessive or X-linked recessive
c) Approximately 98%

Discussion

The incidence of congenital hearing loss (greater than 50 dB) in Western Europe is approximately 1:1,000 live births. In at least 50% of cases the cause is genetic and may be syndromic, autosomal recessive or X-linked recessive. The most common inheritance pattern is autosomal recessive but at least 15 gene loci may be involved in the causation of non-syndromic autosomal recessive hearing loss. The chance of Family A and Family B sharing the same gene defect is small but in the absence of more information an empirical recurrence rate of 12% may be quoted.

Question 3

a) Short PR interval
   Delta wave
b) Symptomatic tachycardia

The most common arrhythmias are a regular atrio-ventricular re-entrant tachycardia and atrial fibrillation, both of which cause symptoms and carry the risk of sudden death.

Question 4

a) Conn's syndrome
Cushing's syndrome
Renal artery stenosis
Congenital adrenal hyperplasia
Diuretic abuse

Any of these would fit this electrolyte pattern.

Question 5

a) Williams syndrome
b) Supravalvular aortic stenosis

Discussion

It is important to be precise with this answer and aortic stenosis alone would not score full marks. Williams syndrome is of unknown aetiology and is associated with hypercalcaemia in infancy.

Cardiac	Supravalvular aortic stenosis
	Peripheral pulmonary artery stenosis
	Pulmonary valve stenosis
Facial	Prominent 'fish' lips
	Blue eyes with stellate pattern in iris
	Short palpebral fissures
Neuro	Developmental delay
	Mild microcephaly

These children tend to be lively and cope well with verbal and social skills but have delayed motor and perceptual abilities. Average IQ 50.

Question 6

a) 7 years
b) Yes

Discussion

Again the question states copy not imitate. These shapes are from the modified Binet and Bender-Gestalt test, and most are used in the Griffiths mental development scales.

By seven years old most children can write their own name.

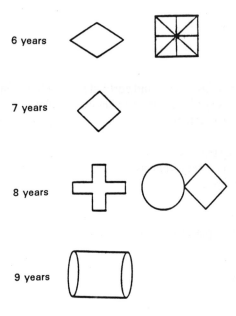

6 years

7 years

8 years

9 years

Question 7

a) Critical pulmonary stenosis
b) Prostaglandin E2
c) Balloon dilatation of pulmonary artery

Question 8

a) ABO incompatibility
b) Maternal anti-A haemolysin

Note that the reticulocyte count is normal for a neonate and that spherocytes are seen in many cases of haemolysis. The positive indirect Coombs test implies the presence of antibodies.

Question 9

a) Whooping cough

Discussion

Causative organism *Bordetella pertussis*. May be cultured in early cases from a nasopharyngeal swab in Bordet-Gengou medium, but is very difficult to isolate once the cough is established.

Diagnosis is largely clinical but a striking absolute lymphocytosis supports the diagnosis.

Serology for complement fixating antibodies. These are nearly always present by the third week.

Complications include bronchopneumonia, bronchiectasis, convulsions and subconjunctival haemorrhages.

Question 10

a) Congenital cyanotic heart disease with right to left shunt

If a normal infant is given more than 80% FiO_2 for more than 10 minutes, the arterial pO_2 should exceed 20 kPa. If pO_2 is below this level, cyanotic heart disease may be present. This is unlikely above 20 kPa and excluded above 27 kPa.

REVISION INDEX